PLAYING THE "COMMUNAL CARD"

Communal Violence and Human Rights

Human Rights Watch

Human Rights Watch
New York • Washington • Los Angeles • London • Brussels

Library of Congress Catalog Card Number: 95-79555
ISBN 1-56432-152-5

Cover photograph: August 19, 1994, Goma, Zaire, courtesy AP/Wide World Photos, Santiago Lyon.

HUMAN RIGHTS WATCH

Human Rights Watch conducts regular, systematic investigations of human rights abuses in some seventy countries around the world. It addresses the human rights practices of governments of all political stripes, of all geopolitical alignments, and of all ethnic and religious persuasions. In internal wars it documents violations by both governments and rebel groups. Human Rights Watch defends freedom of thought and expression, due process and equal protection of the law; it documents and denounces murders, disappearances, torture, arbitrary imprisonment, exile, censorship and other abuses of internationally recognized human rights.

Human Rights Watch began in 1978 with the founding of its Helsinki division. Today, it includes five divisions covering Africa, the Americas, Asia, the Middle East, as well as the signatories of the Helsinki accords. It also includes five collaborative projects on arms transfers, children's rights, free expression, prison conditions, and women's rights. It maintains offices in New York, Washington, Los Angeles, London, Brussels, Moscow, Belgrade, Zagreb, Dushanbe, and Hong Kong. Human Rights Watch is an independent, nongovernmental organization, supported by contributions from private individuals and foundations worldwide. It accepts no government funds, directly or indirectly.

The staff includes Kenneth Roth, executive director; Cynthia Brown, program director; Holly J. Burkhalter, advocacy director; Ann S. Johnson, development director; Gara LaMarche, associate director; Juan Méndez, general counsel; Susan Osnos, communications director; and Derrick Wong, finance and administration director.

The regional directors of Human Rights Watch are Abdullahi An-Na'im, Africa; José Miguel Vivanco, Americas; Sidney Jones, Asia; Jeri Laber, Helsinki; and Christopher E. George, Middle East. The project directors are Joost R. Hiltermann, Arms Project; Lois Whitman, Children's Rights Project; Gara LaMarche, Free Expression Project; and Dorothy Q. Thomas, Women's Rights Project.

The members of the board of directors are Robert L. Bernstein, chair; Adrian W. DeWind, vice chair; Roland Algrant, Lisa Anderson, Peter D. Bell, Alice L. Brown, William Carmichael, Dorothy Cullman, Irene Diamond, Edith Everett, Jonathan Fanton, Alan Finberg, Jack Greenberg, Alice H. Henkin, Harold Hongju Koh, Stephen L. Kass, Marina Pinto Kaufman, Alexander MacGregor, Josh Mailman, Peter Osnos, Kathleen Peratis, Bruce Rabb, Orville Schell, Gary G. Sick, Malcolm Smith, Nahid Toubia, Maureen White, and Rosalind C. Whitehead.

Addresses for Human Rights Watch
485 Fifth Avenue, New York, NY 10017-6104
Tel: (212) 972-8400, Fax: (212) 972-0905, E-mail: hrwnyc@hrw.org

1522 K Street, N.W., #910, Washington, DC 20005-1202
Tel: (202) 371-6592, Fax: (202) 371-0124, E-mail: hrwdc@hrw.org

10951 West Pico Blvd., #203, Los Angeles, CA 90064-2126
Tel: (310) 475-3070, Fax: (310) 475-5613, E-mail: hrwatchla@igc.apc.org

33 Islington High Street, N1 9LH London, UK
Tel: (171) 713-1995, Fax: (171) 713-1800, E-mail: hrwatchuk@gn.apc.org

15 Rue Van Campenhout, 1040 Brussels, Belgium
Tel: (2) 732-2009, Fax: (2) 732-0471, E-mail: hrwatcheu@gn.apc.org

Gopher Address: gopher.humanrights.org port 5000

ACKNOWLEDGEMENTS

Contributors to this report include:
Aziz Abu-Hamad, Cynthia Brown, Holly Cartner, Rachel Denber, Alison Des Forges, Christopher George, Eric Goldstein, Jeannine Guthrie, Farhad Karim, Bronwen Manby, Ivana Nizich, Binaifer Nowrojee, Christopher Panico, Ken Roth and Karen Sorenson.

Cynthia Brown and Farhad Karim edited the report. Nandi Rodrigo provided production assistance.

CONTENTS

INTRODUCTION vii

RWANDA 1

INDIA 18

ISRAELI-OCCUPIED TERRITORIES 30

SOUTH AFRICA 45

ROMANIA 67

SRI LANKA 80

KENYA 97

FORMER YUGOSLAVIA 113

LEBANON 126

ARMENIA-AZERBAIJAN 142

INTRODUCTION

The current epidemic of communal violence—violence involving groups that define themselves by their differences of religion, ethnicity, language or race—is today's paramount human rights problem.[1] The murder of unarmed civilians based on their ethnic, racial or religious affiliations, the forcible displacement of ethnic and religious communities, and the burden that this tragedy places on international humanitarian agencies and donor nations, are now central issues of international relations.

There is broad recognition that early warning and prevention of communal violence are preferable to later, more expensive and generally less effective actions like the U.N. operations in Bosnia and Somalia. Yet because the international community often has not recognized when conflicts framed in ethnic or religious terms are the products of calculated government policies, it has failed to expose and confront those policies early, before their violent consequences explode. Among policies that fuel communal violence are those that reinforce intolerance and excuse harassment of targeted communities, as well as active governmental promotion or direction of violence against those communities. Condemning these official actions as human rights abuses, and treating them as dangers with international significance, must be central to any plan for preventing the outbreak of communal violence.

Communal violence is often seen simply as the product of "deep-seated hatreds" or "ancient animosities" that have been unleashed by the collapse of authoritarian structures that had previously contained them. At times, this view is promoted by journalists who lack the time or inclination to trace more complex causes. Governments presiding over communal violence may also promote this view, since if "ancient animosities" are seen as the "cause", then communal violence takes on the appearance of a natural phenomenon which outsiders have no right to condemn and no hope to prevent. Some members of the international community have also conspired in this view, since inaction in the face of communal violence is more easily excused if the source of that violence is understood to be beyond control.

---

[1] The term "communal conflict" originated in colonial analyses of religious conflicts in the Indian subcontinent. We use the term "communal violence" here to encompass the breadth of the phenomenon, including violent conflict and repression that target communities based not only on their ethnic identities but also their religious affiliation or their racial, linguistic or tribal characteristics.

But the extensive Human Rights Watch field research summarized in this report shows that communal tensions per se are not the immediate cause of many of today's violent and persistent communal conflicts. While communal tensions are obviously a necessary ingredient of an explosive mix, they are not sufficient to unleash widespread violence. Rather, time after time, proximate cause of communal violence is governmental exploitation of communal differences.

The governmental role can take several forms. In some cases, discrimination that favors a dominant group, or marginalizes a minority from full participation in the society, creates a climate of mutual suspicion and intolerance, and the illusion that one group "deserves" more rights than another. The resulting differential in status can breed violent resentment on one hand while inciting, or being seen to excuse, more violent forms of repression on the other. In this climate, when private attacks on a vulnerable community occur, the government may fail to condemn, let alone prosecute, the offenders. Such attacks may even be carried out by official forces, with similar impunity. If the targeted community protests, that is considered further evidence of its posing a threat or being alien to the interests of the state, and can lead to intensified repression.

In other cases, we have seen that a government's willingness to play on existing communal tensions to entrench its own power or advance a political agenda is a key factor in the transformation of those tensions into communal violence. The "communal card" is frequently played, for example, when a government is losing popularity or legitimacy, and finds it convenient to wrap itself in a cloak of ethnic, racial or religious rhetoric. This was the case in Rwanda one year ago. In the spring of 1994, a small group of Rwandan politicians, in an attempt to maintain their control of the government, directed fellow Hutu—the overwhelming ethnic majority in the country—to kill any and all members of the Tutsi minority, as well as Hutu moderates, who were also seen as a threat to their power. These members and allies of the government of Juvenal Habyarimana sought to destroy the support base of the oncoming rebel army of the Rwanda Patriotic Front (RPF), a predominantly Tutsi force. Arming militias composed only of Hutu, and using the state media and allied private media to inflame long-standing anti-Tutsi feeling, this Hutu political group had prepared a climate of extreme communal tension over a period of several years, and the government itself had organized four massacres of Tutsi in 1991-93. When Habyarimana died in a plane crash on April 6, 1994, these politicians blamed the RPF, probably falsely, and instructed Hutu to seek vengeance. The Presidential Guard, as well as government-trained paramilitary militia and thousands of Hutu citizens, slaughtered the country's Tutsi population. Members of the Hutu opposition were also killed. Local officials led the attacks in many cases, targeting victims from lists prepared in advance. In this way, between 500,000 and one million Tutsi of all ages and stations were executed in the space of three months.

The Rwandan genocide did not have to occur, even given the intensity of anti-Tutsi feeling among Hutu in Rwanda. Governmental incitement provided the deadly spark. And warning signs of the government's intent were abundant. Moreover, once the killing began, the international community could have reacted more quickly had the origins of the slaughter been better understood. For while little can be done to stop two entire populations from killing each other, the relatively small group that was orchestrating the genocide could readily have been identified and stopped. But for the first six weeks at least, the international press and influential international leaders persisted in ignoring the manipulative aspect of the slaughter, just as foreign powers had ignored earlier massacres and had even contrived to aid the Habyarimana regime. Still today, it is common to see the Rwandan genocide mistakenly described in press accounts as a spontaneous ethnic war.

When opportunism and the quest for short-term political gains drive governments to foment communal tensions, this should serve as a warning to the international community to take immediate and decisive action. In such circumstances, vulnerable communities need international protection, in the form of pressure on the national government to change divisive and discriminatory policies. Given the governmental origins of much communal violence, early recognition and response by the international community, and support for non-polarizing policies and efforts to defuse tensions, can have a crucial positive effect. The consequences of promoting communal violence—deaths, displacement, starvation, torture—are human rights violations, for which the pertinent government's officials are responsible. As acts of murder and assault, they should be prosecuted under national law, as well as publicly discussed and examined in the interests of political reform. As violations of international human rights law and humanitarian law, they should be exposed, censured and, when necessary, prosecuted by the international community.

In this report Human Rights Watch, which monitors human rights abuses in some seventy countries worldwide, explores governmental provocation of ethnic, racial and religious conflict. Our field research is represented here by studies of communal violence and its relationship to official policies in Rwanda, India, the Israeli Occupied Territories, South Africa, Romania, Sri Lanka, Kenya, the former Yugoslavia, Lebanon, and Azerbaijan. These studies are clearly not intended to exhaust the subject; they are brief essays on complicated situations, intended to highlight facts we believe are often overlooked.

We focus here on cases in which communal violence is centrally directed, either by the state or by others recognized as a coherent leadership by those committing the abuses. In the countries that we examine, the victims and/or the perpetrators of the violence are defined along ethnic, religious or racial lines. In addition, either the government or a major political group pursues violence against a targeted community as a means to achieve a political objective, or the government permits impunity for those engaging in abusive behavior against a targeted group. There are many examples of communal violence that we consider serious, including xenophobic attacks and racist violence in Western Europe and the United States, which have not been included because there was not currently an adequate governmental role in fomenting or systematically tolerating the violence in question to warrant inclusion.[2]

Communal violence has, in some cases, been directed or promoted by a government against a community within its national borders, as in Kenya, Romania and India. Elsewhere, it has been directed against an external community or government, as with the Soviet government's involvement in the conflict over the Nagorno-Karabakh region of Azerbaijan, which is a communal conflict fought for control of territory.

Throughout, we examine conflicts which are commonly described in media accounts and policy debates in terms of bi-polar ethnicity, as if each group's identity were fixed, immutable, and exclusive by definition. Of course, there is an element of truth to this view, since violence tends to sharpen communal differences, as do disenfranchisement and other forms of discrimination that fall short of violence but sow the seeds of it. At the same time, the issue of identity is highly complex. No group can be defined by a single racial, religious or ethnic characteristic, just as no human being is

---

[2] In 1990 and 1991, the German government was slow to recognize the seriousness of acts of violence against foreigners and non-ethnic Germans. The government even used anti-foreigner feelings to forward its political objective of limiting the constitutionally protected right to asylum. In 1993 and 1994, however, the government adopted measures to combat and punish "skinhead" violence, and these have led to more thorough investigations, more vigorous prosecutions and heavier sentences for these crimes. Nonetheless, the extent of ethnically directed violence is still four times higher than in 1991, and violent anti-Semitic attacks, as well as attacks on socially marginal groups such as the homeless, homosexuals and the disabled, have been increasing rapidly.

ethnically "pure" and no society exists that does not have its minorities. In many situations, ethnic identity has traditionally been fluid, such that over time the issue of difference has been resolved by one group's blending into another for accommodation. In Rwanda, prior to the twentieth century and intervention by Europeans, Hutu and Tutsi were not ethnic definitions at all but labels for changeable economic status: one was Hutu when poor, and could become Tutsi when more prosperous.

A similar fluidity can be found in the traditional movement—both upward and downward—among castes in India; in the emergence of an ethnically pluralist national identity in Yugoslavia prior to its division; and in mixed marriages the world over. Political allegiance may also be fluid—as, witness, in Bosnia, where some Serbs of Sarajevo have sought to uphold a pluralistic society by siding with the predominantly Muslim Bosnian government, or the complex cross-hatching of political and ethnic loyalties in Lebanon and Sri Lanka, or the way that Somali sub-clans, over a generation, may expediently shift loyalty from one clan grouping to another in their vicinity. Even in highly politicized situations, when communal identities become more rigid, there is typically an element of any ethnic, religious or racial community—often a large proportion of the community—that favors pluralism and negotiation rather than conflict.

The Role of Governments

Governments at times play the "communal card" by directing agents of the state to commit acts of violence, as in Rwanda and the "ethnic cleansing" underway in Bosnia. Governments also frequently arm segments of the population to act in the government's short-term political interests. Again, Rwanda is a case in point. But similarly, in Sri Lanka during the past decade, "home guards" armed and perfunctorily trained by the government, supposedly for civil defense of non-Tamil ethnic communities, engaged in massacres of neighboring Tamil villagers while security forces in the vicinity stood by. And recently in Kenya, the Moi government created and trained the so-called "Kalenjin warriors" to unleash terror, provoke displacement and impose control over the majority Kikuyu of the fertile, politically important Rift Valley.

The dissemination of communal antipathy through the state media often plays a central role in promoting violence, especially when official media have a monopoly. Equally effective can be censorship of media that oppose the state's role in communal violence. Serb radio in Bosnia broadcast propaganda for a "Greater Serbia," as well as misinformation about Muslims and the multi-ethnic Bosnian government, in areas under Bosnian Serb control. Meanwhile, Serbian authorities in Belgrade censored their own press, ensured that Serbian citizens who opposed the war could not obtain adequate time in state-owned media to express their opinions, and prevented independent radio from broadcasting outside the greater Belgrade area. From purges of dissident journalists in Serbia to jamming of Croatian and Bosnian television, Serbian authorities maintained control over the content of news reaching audiences in Serbia and in Serb-held areas of Bosnia.[3]

Some governments favor or promote parties or private groups driven by a communal agenda, and tolerate the violence these groups or parties commit, in order to pursue political goals without openly using state power. Practitioners of this strategy are legion: in this volume alone, we examine the former Rwandan government's arming of militia; the apartheid government of South Africa's covert promotion of the Inkatha Freedom Party; the support of Hindu nationalist groups by Indian governments since Indira Gandhi; the Israeli government's discriminatory tolerance of violence by settlers in the Occupied Territories; and the Sri Lankan government of the 1980s, which appropriated some of the rival Tamil separatist groups to undertake counterinsurgency in Tamil-speaking areas, sometimes alongside government forces but often on their own.

Communal tensions also tend to rise when a government defines political rights in terms of communities rather than individuals. While granting privileges to disadvantaged or minority communities can address inequities, representation that is based merely on communal identity, rather than on the free choice of individuals, gives the ostensible leaders of communities excessive power and locks communities into perpetual competition on communal lines. In Lebanon, government positions and other benefits have been apportioned to officially recognized sects and distributed through sectarian leaders for the past fifty years; in order to preserve the privileges the system brings them, sectarian leaders have incited communal violence, controlled information, restricted human rights and invited outside intervention.

---

[3] An instructive recent variation on this tactic was a well coordinated campaign of misinformation and intimidation carried out with leaflets and over state radio in Burma between December 1994 and March 1995. With the apparent intent to terrorize Buddhist refugees and set the pluralist Karen separatist movement against itself, the state radio and leaflets distributed in the refugee camps reported as fact the allegation that Buddhists and Christians within the rebel movement were carrying out pogroms against each others' supporters. Some leaflets even called on Buddhist Karens to kill the Christian leader of the Karen army. A climate of suspicion and fear has resulted in which both groups are wary and some Buddhist refugees have even returned to Burma, to escape expected Christian attacks.

State involvement in communal violence is not always direct. A government may encourage communal violence through tolerance of it, as when officials systematically fail to prosecute or publicly condemn acts of harassment and violence against a targeted community. The Romanian government's persistent failure to bring anyone to trial for the torching of Roma (Gypsy) homes and wholesale violence against Roma communities in the past several years is, in this respect, analogous to the Indian government's tolerance of Hindu nationalists' violence against Muslims.

Failure to prosecute acts of communal violence is perceived as tacit approval and thus encourages abusive behavior. In this way governments send the message that members of a vulnerable community deserve less respect and will receive less protection than other citizens. Whether the perpetrator is a soldier or a member of a private group, the message of impunity is the same so long as the state does not punish crimes and provide equal protection to all its citizens. Bringing perpetrators to account is, therefore, one of the most important steps that can be taken to deter communal violence.

It is difficult to make political generalizations about societies that encourage communal violence. Governments as different as those of Cambodia, Ethiopia and Russia all pursue policies that have provoked or promoted communal violence—including official tolerance of attacks against the ethnic Vietnamese under the Royal Government of Cambodia, against minority clan groups within the ethnically defined regions that make up Ethiopia's experiment in "ethnic federalism," and against minority ethnic communities in post-Soviet Russia. Class differences do not necessarily define victims or abusers: where the community of potential victims is large, as with Muslims in India, attackers do not necessarily favor rich over poor or vice versa. Nor are victims even necessarily members of a minority community: the Iraqi government of Saddam Hussein systematically represses the Shi'a majority, favoring his minority Sunni sect;[4] in the area now officially Bosnia-Hercegovina, Muslims, the principal

---

[4] The government of Iraq has targeted Shi'a cultural and other nonpolitical institutions in order to eradicate the foundations of Shi'a society. These attacks have included the closure, confiscation and destruction of Shi'a mosques, schools, cemeteries and centers. In March 1991, over one hundred clerics were detained in the Shi'a cities of Kerbala and Najaf. To date there is no official word of their whereabouts, although they are believed to be alive in detention. In southern Iraq, under the guise of security concerns, the government has drained the marshes where Shi'a (also known as Marsh Arabs) live, sent in the military with tanks to attack and burn the inhabitants' reed dwellings, and scattered the survivors.

victims of "ethnic cleansing," have been a plurality for centuries.

But dictatorship offers the ideal condition for playing the "communal card." Under a dictatorship, official control of information makes public opinion highly manipulable, while the state's suppression of dissent facilitates reprisals against anyone officially defined as an ethnic, religious or racial "enemy." In an extreme case, genocide can be efficiently organized and disguised. To carry out the genocidal Anfal campaign of 1988, Iraqi government soldiers exterminated tens of thousands of noncombatant Iraqi Kurds, destroyed 2,000 Kurdish villages, jailed and warehoused noncombatants in conditions of extreme deprivation in which hundreds died, and forced the displacement of hundreds of thousands of villagers, who were trucked far from home and, abandoned without aid of any kind, forbidden to return. All this was accomplished in less than seven months. The Iraqi government used euphemisms like "executive measures" to conceal the facts of the Anfal, and no independent source of information was available at the time to expose the truth.

Where political debate and information on communal issues are controlled, advocates of ethnic or religious exclusion are more likely to thrive uncontradicted. Similarly, in the absence of a vibrant civil society, a government will meet with less criticism when it fails to apply the law to groups acting violently in the name of communal "purity." In South Africa, the apartheid regime covertly funded, armed and tolerated violence by the self-described Zulu party, the Inkatha Freedom Party, in order to promote the IFP's conflict with the African National Congress and thus to weaken the ANC as a multi-ethnic force for change. Only beginning in 1993 as elections neared and the society opened up was it possible to expose the apartheid government's use of the IFP.

If communal violence is most easily fomented in a closed society, the obverse is also true: a well developed civil society permits people to have a civic identity which is not limited to ethnicity, race or religion. Conditions for polarization along communal lines are less propitious in a society where public debate is encouraged, where members of diverse communities have equal rights as citizens of the nation, and where diverse ethnic, racial and religious communities are broadly represented in the media, the armed forces and police, the government sector, education, and other public institutions. These conditions reflect respect for basic rights set out in international human rights instruments, including the right to political participation, the right to free expression and association, and the right to be treated without discrimination based on race, religion or ethnicity.

Not only governments but also rebel groups may be guilty of communal violence, in violation of international humanitarian law. Tamil separatists in Sri Lanka, notably the Liberation Tigers of Tamil Eelam (LTTE), have engaged in political violence and large-scale massacres of Muslim and Sinhalese civilians, and in 1990 the LTTE forced the wholesale eviction of Muslims from areas of northern Sri Lanka under their control. In Rwanda, some RPF forces massacred several hundred civilians during their military advance, evidently in retaliation for the genocide carried out against the Tutsi. Clearly such practices, like the conduct of governments, should be subject to prosecution under national law and to accountability under international law.

Human Rights Watch does not condemn the formation or existence of civil organizations or political parties based on religion or ethnic affiliation. These should be protected by the right of free association. But if a group with an ethnic, religious or racial agenda becomes a government, it takes on the duty to abide by international covenants that require the protection of all citizens' safety and physical integrity, right to due process, ability to participate in the country's political life, and other basic rights. As parties or private groups, these organizations may or may not represent a large constituency. As a government, they are obligated to protect the rights of everyone.

Conclusions and Recommendations

The studies contained in this report, and our regular monitoring of other situations of communal tension and conflict, lead us to certain conclusions about communal violence and recommendations for measures to prevent its proliferation.

(1) Communal violence is often the product of policies that legitimize communal hatred and conflate it with national identity, as when a government

o   encourages one community to attack another, through official statements or instructions or the arming of one community for purposes of attacking others.

o   defines the state, or citizenship, in ethnic, religious, or   racial terms such as to grant less than full rights to persons of other communities.

o   imposes a state religion, state language or state ethnic identity in a manner that grants less than full religious rights or political participation to members of other communities or is calculated to inflame ethnic sensibilities.

o   seeks forcibly to create ethnic enclaves, or to fashion enclaves in which

xv

one ethnic group is legally dominant—both steps that encourage ethnic tension no matter what the government's immediate motivation may be.

(2) Communal violence is often promoted by governments through a pattern of discrimination that is intended to, or can be reasonably expected to, lead to inter-communal conflict. That discrimination can include

o   failure to provide physical protection for vulnerable communities under attack from private actors.

o   failure to prosecute those responsible for attacks on targeted communities, whether these are state agents or private actors.

o   persistent official representation of members of a targeted community, in media and official comments, as less than full citizens or deserving of less than full respect.

o   suppression of dissent by those (of whatever origin) who oppose attacks on or discrimination against the targeted community.

o   discriminatory legislation, which denies full status and recourse to members of the targeted community with regard to their rights as citizens of the nation.[5]

(3) Communal violence is the final stage of a process that often begins with government manipulation of ethnic tensions to polarize public opinion. It is crucial that the initial polarization be avoided if possible or, if not, that the national and international communities take it seriously once violence begins to result. While each national situation is unique and demands individual analysis,

---

[5] International human rights instruments define a right of minorities to preserve their culture. Human Rights Watch, according to its mandate, does not take a position on what measures a government is obliged to adopt to help a community reinforce its cultural identity as a sub-group within the nation. We do, however, oppose prohibitions on a community organizing its own services to reinforce its ethnic, religious or other communal identity, such as the creation of privately funded teaching in the language of the community or the establishment of its own churches.

we believe that polarization may be deterred by the creation of mechanisms that permit the society to confront and change divisive official policies, in particular

o   transparent governmental processes to investigate early instances of violence against targeted groups, culminating in the broad distribution of public reports of findings.

o   criminal prosecutions and public trials for those who order or engage in attacks on targeted communities.

o   government policies that permit vigorous civic debate about how to resolve communal tensions.

o   government policies that permit all citizens free participation in a broad range of voluntary and public associations.

(4) Preventing communal violence is principally the task of national governments. But as these governments are so often complicit in the violence, they cannot be the sole guardians of the welfare of vulnerable communities. Under such international human rights treaties as the Convention on the Prevention and Punishment of the Crime of Genocide, the international community has a clearly defined responsibility to become involved where widespread communal violence is underway or threatened. And given that communal violence has direct and burdensome consequences for neighboring governments and the humanitarian aid budgets of the international community, there are pragmatic as well as moral reasons for intergovernmental organizations, regional organizations and nongovernmental humanitarian and human rights groups to play a central role in monitoring and vigorously condemning policies that lead to polarization of communities, violence between communities, and patterns of discrimination that encourage violence. In particular, the international community should

o   insist on the physical protection of members of vulnerable communities, especially when there is evidence that they face concerted attacks.

o   encourage governments to provide equal protection under the law, and when governments acting in good faith require international technical assistance in fortifying their legal systems to provide effective protection, offer such assistance.

o   speak out against political strategies designed to heighten communal tensions or promote communally exclusive agendas.

o   expect that a government that receives well founded recommendations for reform from a national commission investigating communal violence will accept those recommendations and act accordingly, and if it does not, condemn its failure to do so.

o   seek perspectives on communal issues from nongovernmental sources, including factual information on contemporary abuses, official policy, and local efforts to negotiate or otherwise peacefully resolve communal tensions.

o   protest any government's failure to eliminate official obstacles to equal access to media representation for targeted communities.

o   deny international assistance to, and refrain from steps that tend to legitimize, any government that promotes communal violence in its own or another territory.

RWANDA

In the spring of 1994, a small group of Rwandan politicians pushed communal violence to the level of genocide in a desperate bid to hold onto power. They directed the state and the army to extirpate the Tutsi minority, whom they accused of being "accomplices" of the Rwanda Patriotic Front (RPF) that had invaded the country in October 1990. They also organized the systematic slaughter of thousands of Hutu who were willing to work with the Tutsi to build a new political order. The international community, witness to the genocide of between 500,000 and one million people, intervened only to withdraw foreign nationals.

The RPF ended the genocide by defeating the Rwandan government army in July 1994. The authorities guilty of genocide then led about one million Hutu Rwandans into exile in Zaire, creating a massive humanitarian crisis. Here the international community hurried to the rescue but some 50,000 refugees died nonetheless of disease, hunger and lack of water. The authors of genocide profited from the international humanitarian aid to regroup for further attacks against the RPF-led government. At the same time, they committed flagrant abuses against their fellow Hutu refugees whom they cast as pawns in bargaining with the international community. They used propaganda, intimidation and violence to keep the refugees from returning home.

The RPF was also guilty of committing violations of human rights. Some RPF troops massacred hundreds of civilians at several sites during the course of their advance against the Rwandan army. After the establishment of a coalition government led by the RPF, the new authorities committed themselves to a program of justice and equal rights for all. Thus far, however, they have failed to end recurrent abuses by soldiers of their army (now known as the Rwandan Patriotic Army, or RPA) against the largely Hutu population.

Background

Over the centuries, a variety of peoples settled in Rwanda and created a centralized nation under one ruler, with a single language and a common culture. As the state grew, an aristocratic elite, now known as the Tutsi, assumed increasing control over the mass of the people, who were called Hutu. Lines between the groups were permeable; rich Hutu became Tutsi while Tutsi who lost their wealth could become Hutu.

During the colonial period, which began at the start of the twentieth century, first the Germans, then the Belgians, ruled through the Tutsi, whom they held to be superior to the Hutu. They guaranteed them a monopoly of both political power and higher level education. The European administrators were anxious to define clearly the previously fluid social groups and instituted a system of population registration, recording each person's group affiliation at birth. Each adult was required to carry an identity card including this information. These administrative measures made it almost impossible for Hutu to become Tutsi just at a time when being Tutsi brought all the advantages. The system of identity cards continued after independence, and the documents which had once guaranteed privileges to the Tutsi eventually became the means of selecting them for genocide.

Independence
Throughout most of the colonial period, the Tutsi were assured of the unreserved backing of the colonial administrators, and they used this support to increase their exploitation of the Hutu far beyond what had existed before the European arrival. But in the 1950s, Belgium—which administered Rwanda as a trust territory—came under increasing pressure from the United Nations to prepare to transfer power to a government which had the support of the majority Hutu. They abruptly changed their policy of total support for the Tutsi and obliged them to share power and educational opportunities with the Hutu. The reforms frightened the Tutsi but did not satisfy the Hutu; as independence approached, each group feared that the Belgian departure would leave them at the mercy of the other.

In July 1959, a moderate ruler who had reigned since 1931 died suddenly and was succeeded by a weak conservative. The political scene became increasingly polarized, with moderate parties that included both Hutu and Tutsi losing power to more extreme parties, which were identified with one particular group. In November 1959 the era of communal violence began when Tutsi extremists attacked a Hutu leader. Hutu groups retaliated by killing Tutsi officials. Tutsi administrators unleashed reprisals on the Hutu under their jurisdiction. Only after several hundred people of each group had been killed did the Belgians intervene. They dramatically changed the face of the administration by replacing about half the Tutsi chiefs and sub-chiefs with Hutu ones. With the help of these new administrators, Hutu political parties won the first national elections, held in June 1960. By January 1961 Hutu leaders were strong enough to declare the end of the Tutsi monarchy. The ruler fled to Nairobi. When the Belgians withdrew in July 1962, Rwanda was left an independent republic ruled by the all-Hutu Paramehetu party.

Once firmly in power, many Hutu officials harassed and intimidated Tutsi, particularly those who served in the administration under the Belgians. They seized their cattle and drove them off their lands, either to other parts of the country or to the surrounding countries of Burundi, Zaire, Uganda and Tanzania. In 1961, some of the Tutsi refugees began raiding Rwanda from their host countries. They launched ten major attacks between 1961 and 1966. After each attack, Hutu officials incited reprisals against those Tutsi still in the country, each time widening further the circle of victims until finally everyone labeled Tutsi was at risk, whether or not they had ever held power in the colonial era. The officials did so both to increase their own power and to enable them to appropriate the property of the victims which they could redistribute to win greater support in the community. In the worst such case, following a Tutsi attack from Burundi in December 1963, Hutu killed an estimated 10,000 Tutsi, about half the total of 20,000 said to have been killed during these years. With each episode of violence, more Tutsi left Rwanda. By 1990 those who had fled, together with their children born abroad, numbered between 400,000 and 500,000. While some had been assimilated into the populations of their host countries, most were still awaiting the opportunity to return home.

The Rule of Habyarimana

When refugee attacks came to a stop in 1966, open violence against Tutsi in Rwanda also ended, but the Hutu government continued to discriminate against the Tutsi, particularly in education and employment. In 1973 attacks on the Tutsi resumed, apparently engineered by the military to provide an excuse for a *coup d'etat*. Gen. Juvenal Habyarimana took power, pledging to restore order. For the next twenty years he ruled through his party, the Republican Movement for Democracy and Development (MRND), the only one permitted in the country. At first widely popular with Hutu throughout Rwanda, he lost favor as his years in power stretched out and corruption increased, particularly to the benefit of his immediate associates and his home region of northwestern Rwanda. He also lost support because of economic difficulties beyond his control, caused mostly by the sudden fall in the world market price for coffee, Rwanda's chief export. Under pressure from foreign donors in the late 1980s, Habyarimana initiated economic reforms that had the unintended effect of increasing the suffering of the poorest sector of the population. Also partly as a result of foreign pressure and partly in response to internal demands for change, he began a program of political reforms in 1990 meant to lead to a multiparty system and free elections.

The Rwandan Patriotic Front

In the late 1980s, Rwandan refugees based in Uganda and organized in the Rwandan Patriotic Front pushed increasingly for their right to return home. Most were Tutsi, but they attracted the support of several Hutu who had once been close to Habyarimana but who had since fled Rwanda. They included Col. Alexis Kanyarengwe, who became chairman of the organization, and Pasteur Bizimungu, now president of Rwanda. Many Rwandans who served in the National Resistance

Army that had won power for Yoweri Museveni, the president of Uganda, also joined the RPF. Among them was Gen. Paul Kagame, now vice-president of Rwanda and the commanding officer who led the RPF army to victory. When President Habyarimana appeared weakened by growing internal dissent and economic problems, the RPF decided to attack Rwanda, both to oust Habyarimana and to clear the way for the refugees to return home. On October 1, 1990, about 700,000 RPF soldiers crossed the border into Rwanda. They included several thousand who had deserted from the Ugandan army.

In reaction to the invasion, the Habyarimana government staged a fake attack on its own capital of Kigali. For several hours on the night of October 4, soldiers of the government army fired in the air to create the illusion that the RPF had besieged the city. The next morning, the government used the supposed attack to justify arresting Tutsi, accused of being "accomplices" who "provided cover" for the RPF. They also arrested hundreds of Hutu who were thought to be opponents of Habyarimana. Over the next few weeks between 8,000 and 10,000 people were detained, about 75 percent of whom were Tutsi. They were held without charge in deplorable conditions, many for months before their release. Many were tortured and dozens were killed.

The Government of Rwanda and Communal Violence

Two weeks after the invasion, the government organized a massacre of Tutsi. This campaign, which slaughtered some 350 people in the northwestern commune of Kibirira, was the first in more than twenty years and resembled the reprisal killings that took place during the invasions of the 1960s. It, in turn, established a pattern found in three subsequent massacres launched over the next months—in northwestern Rwanda in January and February 1991, in Bugesera in March 1992, and again in the northwest in December 1992 and January 1993—and in the great genocide of April 1994.

In each case, the government prepared for the massacre by creating fear of the Tutsi. In Kibirira, officials falsely reported at public meetings that Tutsi infiltrators had been found and killed in the immediate area. At the time of the slaughter in the northwest in early 1991, the army once more used the trick of a fake attack staged on a military camp in the region. At the time of the Bugesera massacres, the national radio broadcast false news bulletins about Tutsi plans to kill Hutu. At the end of December 1992, officials warned people near Gishwati forest that killers lurked in the bushes and that they needed to get rid of them.

In the first massacres, the officials themselves directed the killings. In Kibirira they told Hutu to kill their Tutsi neighbors to fulfill their *umuganda* obligation for the month. (Umuganda, a duty carried over from the colonial era, consisted of one day per month of unpaid labor for public service projects, like repairing roads or building schools.) With the early 1991 slaughter in the northwest, both civilian and military authorities directed the operations. In one case, the local official had a number of the victims buried in the back yard of his house. Just as authorities began the violence, so they could stop it. In Kibirira, they sent two policemen who halted the killings just by blowing their whistles and giving the order to disperse.

By the time of the attacks in Bugesera, in March 1992, the authorities had found it necessary to adapt their tactics because of growing criticism of their human rights abuses. Rather than take the clear lead in killing Tutsi, they shared responsibility with leaders of new militia organizations. The militia, known as the Interahamwe (Those Who Stand Together), were armed groups attached to the MRND, the political party headed by President Habyarimana himself. Although the militia were clearly acting as a tool of the state, the authorities apparently hoped to convince the international community that they were really independent actors. By thus "privatizing" the violence, they sought to deflect criticism of the Habyarimana government.

Once the killing campaigns had begun, local authorities refused to issue the permits needed to move from one commune to another, thus making it impossible for potential victims to flee to safety or to disseminate news of the massacres. In Bugesera, soldiers herded victims together and disarmed them, leaving them prey to civilian assailants. In the northwest, militia manned barriers that blocked movement from one area to another.

In each case, the attacks began either with the burning of houses and looting of property or with isolated assaults on a few people. When these small beginnings attracted little notice, the authorities were encouraged to extend the attacks, both in range and in gravity. In the end, several hundred people were killed in each case.

After the slaughter of the Bagogwe, a subgroup of the Tutsi, in the northwest in January-February 1991, the government refused to acknowledge the killings. It asserted instead that the victims had all simply disappeared, most of them fled to join the ranks of the RPF. Because the Bagogwe were slaughtered in a region near the battlefront, where access was controlled by the military, the government expected to be able to prevent any inquiries that would reveal the truth. But in January 1993, the nongovernmental International Commission on Human Rights Abuse in Rwanda, sponsored by Human Rights Watch/Africa and three other international human rights organizations, collected abundant testimony and material evidence about these massacres.

In the other three cases, the government did not deny that the killings had taken place but sought to explain them as the result of spontaneous, uncontrollable rage against and fear of the Tutsi. Well aware of the susceptibility of foreigners to explanations of "ancient, tribal hatreds" among Africans, they repeatedly underlined the supposedly "tribal" nature of the killings in an effort to mask the deliberate role played by the authorities.

The four massacres carried out between October 1990 and February 1993 took the lives of some 2,000 victims, most of them Tutsi, injured hundreds of others and drove thousands more from their homes. Some government officials were removed from their posts following the massacres, but no one, either official or ordinary citizen, was convicted of any crime in connection with these attacks.

The Role of the International Community

Foreign powers, so important in distorting and embittering relations between Tutsi and Hutu in the colonial period, also played a role in more recent cases of communal conflict. Heavily involved in supporting the Habyarimana government—responsible for about 60 percent of its annual budget—donor nations at first ignored evidence of its role in inciting and directing communal violence. When called to aid the Rwandan government in the face of the RPF invasion, both France and Belgium sent troops. Belgium withdrew its soldiers soon after, but French troops stayed for nearly three years, supposedly training Rwandan soldiers but in fact also supporting them in combat. France continued to supply financial aid and to assist in arms sales to the government, even when massacres perpetrated by the authorities had been criticized within Rwanda and abroad. Egypt and South Africa also ignored the Rwandan record of human rights abuses and continued to sell arms to the government.

When the nongovernmental International Human Rights Commission published its report in March 1993 clearly implicating the Habyarimana government in numerous and systematic human rights abuses, including inciting communal violence, Belgium reacted by recalling its ambassador. The United States both reduced its aid and redirected much of the remainder from the Rwandan government to nongovernmental organizations. The report was also presented to the United Nations Human Rights Commission, which chose not to act at the time.

The international community hesitated to act directly on the problem of communal violence, but it was anxious for the war to be ended. During the summer of 1993, it exerted considerable pressure on the Rwandan government to come to terms with the RPF. The government, by this time a coalition of Habyarimana's MRND and several opposition parties, signed the Arusha Accords with the RPF on August 4. The accords provided for a transitional government, with power to be shared among the Habyarimana faction, the internal opposition, and the RPF. During the twenty-two months that the transitional government was to prepare for elections, a United Nations peacekeeping force, called UNAMIR, was to contribute to the security of the capital, protect opposition leaders as well as RPF troops stationed in Kigali, and facilitate the integration of the two armies.

From Communal Violence to Genocide

President Habyarimana and his supporters, dissatisfied with the terms of the accords and panicked at the prospect of losing power, decided very soon after signing the agreement not to implement it. To slow the installation of the transitional government, they fomented divisions within the opposition political parties, a maneuver which succeeded partly because of the greed and opportunism of some of their leaders. At the same time, the Habyarimana group began preparations for pushing communal violence to its most extreme form, genocide.

The basic accusation that all Tutsi were "accomplices" of the RPF, first enunciated soon after the October 1990 invasion, was spelled out in detail in a November 1992 speech by Leon Mugesera, a favorite of Habyarimana and an important political figure in northwestern Rwanda. Speaking at a site near the Kibirira massacre, Mugesera developed the idea that Tutsi were aliens, interlopers from Ethiopia, who had no rights in Rwanda. He exhorted the crowd to send them back home by the shortest possible route, a river that fed into the Nile. It went without saying that they were to be killed before being dumped in the river. His demand to send all the Tutsi back "home" was the first recorded statement of the genocidal intent to rid Rwanda completely of this group. Later propaganda stressed the cleverness of the Tutsi and insisted that they would somehow manage to gain mastery of the country and re-institute the repressive regime of the colonial era. Hutu were taught that the RPF, aided by Tutsi within the country, were planning to exterminate them and that a preemptive attack was the only way to save their own lives. They were told that it had been a mistake to spare Tutsi children in earlier massacres because they had grown up to pose a new threat to Hutu. This time, Hutu were told, even babies must be exterminated.

The primary voice of genocide was the Radio Television Libre des Mille Collines (RTLM), a private radio station organized by Habyarimana's wife, her brothers and other cronies of the president. It began broadcasting shortly after the Arusha Accords were signed in August 1993. At the time of the Bugesera massacre in March 1992, Radio Rwanda broadcasts had shown the effectiveness of the radio in reaching large numbers of potential assailants. But, perhaps in reaction to international criticism, the government had decided to privatize the incitements to violence, much as it had privatized the execution of the killings through the creation of the militia. The link between the national radio and the new private station was made clear by the appointment of Ferdinand Nahimana as its first director. Responsible for Radio Rwanda when it was used to incite the Bugesera massacre, Nahimana had been removed following international criticism. At the head of RTLM, Nahimana began broadcasting an increasingly virulent torrent of accusations against Tutsi in general and Hutu members of the opposition willing to work with them. The radio targeted leading politicians, like Minister of Labor and Social Affairs, Landouald Ndasingwa, and members of civil society, like human rights activist Monique Mujawamariya. It exhorted listeners to rid the country of these "traitors," by whatever means necessary.

The Habyarimana group recruited unemployed young men for the Interahamwe militia, which had proved its usefulness in the massacres in Bugesera in 1992 and in the northwest in early 1993. Close allies of Habyarimana, organized in the political party called the Coalition for the Defense of the Republic (CDR), also recruited members for a militia called the Impuzamugambi (Those With a Single Purpose). The young recruits were trained in groups of 300 at a time by soldiers of the Rwandan army. The three-week training programs were carried out at military camps distant from the capital. The militia members were paid a small salary and given distinctive clothes. At first these were only caps and shirts, but as the units proved their usefulness, they were rewarded with fashionable jogging suits.

Beginning in 1991, the Rwandan government handed out guns free to citizens in areas near the frontier as part of a "self-defense" program against the enemy. By the end of 1993, arms were being distributed so widely that the Catholic bishop of Nyundo protested in a pastoral letter, asking what was the point of the armament campaign. Grenades were also given free to members of the militia and others known to favor Habyarimana's position. Grenades had the potential of killing large numbers of people quickly and had the additional advantage of requiring little training for their use. In January and February 1994, the Habyarimana faction attempted to import several large shipments of arms in violation of the peace accords. UNAMIR intervened and the effort failed, but the authorities apparently still had plenty to arm increasing numbers of supporters during the early months of 1994. Once the large-scale killing had begun in April, the Habyarimana group were able to distribute even more firearms to the assailants, including automatic and semi-automatic rifles and pistols.

In February 1994 two leading politicians were assassinated, one opposed to Habyarimana and the other, a Habyarimana loyalist. The Interahamwe militia then killed scores of people and closed down government offices in the capital city. UNAMIR shifted some troops from outlying areas into the capital, but otherwise did not intervene to stop the escalating violence. By March, activists and highly placed government officials were warning diplomats in Kigali as well as international organizations like Human Rights Watch that the killing campaign was about to be launched. Some of those targeted sent their children away, but most took no measures to protect themselves or their families because they believed UNAMIR would protect them.

After months of preparation, the genocide was touched off by the death of President Habyarimana in a plane crash on April 6. Habyarimana was en route home after an international conference in Tanzania where progress had apparently been made on actually implementing the long-discussed transitional government. The plane was downed by ground fire from positions near the airport, a region controlled by the Rwandan army. This evidence substantiated accusations that some of Habyarimana's own soldiers had been responsible for killing him. But Hutu extremists promptly accused the RPF of the attack and used the accusation to justify launching their long-planned slaughter of Hutu opponents and genocide of the Tutsi.

The authors of the genocide were a small circle of the most powerful people in Rwanda, some of whom held military or civilian positions, others of whom exercised power informally through their personal ties to Habyarimana. This group operated initially through the Presidential Guard, an elite force attached to Habyarimana, and through the Interahamwe and Impuzamugambi militia. Several days after the crash, the extremists installed a rump government that purported to represent a number of political parties and thus to continue the mandate of the previous coalition government. In fact all the "ministers" emerged from the same ideological position, whatever their party labels, and the government existed only to give a cover of legitimacy to the killing campaigns. The "president" of this self-proclaimed government was Theodore Sindikubwabo, the "prime minister" was Jean Kambanda, and the commander-in-chief was Col. Augustin Bizimungu. Once in full command of the state, they used the civilian administration and the regular army hierarchy to direct the genocide. In one case after another, the local government officials led the attacks, usually operating from lists that had been prepared ahead of time. In such places as the commune of Nyakizu in southern Rwanda, local officials and other killers came "to work" every morning. After they had put in a full day of "work" killing Tutsi, they "went home, singing" at quitting time, according to what one witness told Human Rights Watch/Africa. The "workers" returned each day until the job had been finished--that is, until all the Tutsi had been killed. These methodical massacres were only the amplification of killings at Kibirira nearly four years before, when killing had first been qualified as the public obligation of umuganda.

In many communities, soldiers of the Rwandan army accompanied groups of civilian killers to reinforce their will and to give more concrete assistance, if need be. At the site of the massacre at Nyarubuye Church, Human Rights Watch/Africa found military supplies indicating that Rwandan army soldiers had participated in the slaughter there.

After ten weeks of genocidal killings, Colonel Bizimungu told the United Nations human rights special rapporteur that his government could stop the slaughter but would not until the RPF agreed to a ceasefire.

In mobilizing Hutu to attack the Tutsi, the officials exploited fears generated by the months of propaganda, particularly that broadcast on the radio. They also played upon the greed of the poor by promising them control of the land and houses of the victims, as well as movable property looted from them. Hutu who still hesitated to participate in the massacres might themselves face death. Dr. Rony Zacharias of Médecins sans Frontières testified at the May 25, 1994, meeting of the U.N. Human Rights Commission that he had seen militia arrive with a truckload of machetes at the Butare hospital and tell Hutu staff members "Kill or be killed." In cases like these, the immediate fear of death or injury at the hands of other Hutu came to replace the more distant fear of eventual attack by the Tutsi.

Within an hour of the plane crash, the Presidential Guard and the militia had installed the first barriers in the city of Kigali to stop the flight of intended victims. The next morning a complete curfew was imposed, making it impossible for people to leave their homes. By the time the curfew was eased during daylight hours, roadblocks and barriers had been established throughout the country. Victims were left with few choices. Those who sought to flee were stopped at the barriers and asked for their identity cards. Virtually all those identified as Tutsi were taken to the side of the road and killed. Some chose to remain at home, where a fortunate few managed to survive by hiding in underground holes or between the rafters and the roof of their houses. Some assembled in a local center, such as a church, school or hospital, that had served as a place of refuge in the past. Those who did so presented the most tempting targets to the assailants, an opportunity to kill the maximum number with the least expenditure of energy and resources. Even places of worship, recognized as sanctuaries throughout the world, provided no security: assailants threw grenades in through windows, forced doors, and slaughtered unarmed civilians even at the foot of the altar.

In some communities, Tutsi decided to resist the attacks and defended themselves successfully for several days or even weeks. But the resisters had few weapons and were prevented by the barriers from getting outside help while the assailants had ample weapons and could bring in unlimited reinforcements, including soldiers of the regular army and the Presidential Guard. In regions of southern and central Rwanda, Hutu sometimes joined with Tutsi in trying to fight off the attackers. But when it became clear that the genocidal killers would prevail, most of Hutu fled or joined the assailants.

The massacres, launched swiftly and with great organization, took hundreds of lives within the first day. But a prompt and effective international reaction could have limited the violence. Unfortunately the only prompt and effective operation mounted by the international community was the rescue of foreign nationals, which was carried out with great success soon after the killing began.

UNAMIR, although charged with contributing to the security of the capital, was limited by a restrictive mandate that did not permit its troops to fire except in self-defense. Small patrols sent to protect opposition political leaders either fled, as did the group assigned to protect Minister Landaould Ndasingwa, or laid down their arms and were themselves slaughtered—as were ten Belgian soldiers sent to rescue the Prime Minister Agathe Uwilingiyimana. The Belgians, panicked by the brutal torture and killing of their soldiers, withdrew their troops from UNAMIR. Because these soldiers were the best equipped and trained of the force, their withdrawal dealt a serious blow to the U.N. peacekeeping efforts. Other nations followed the Belgian lead because they believed that as the former colonial power, it knew the region best. No serious effort was made to find another nation willing to replace the withdrawn Belgian soldiers. Even without additional troops, the UNAMIR force already on the spot could have saved countless civilian lives had its mandate been strengthened to permit it to act. Rather than do so, the Security Council left the mandate unchanged and, two weeks after the genocide began, reduced the force from 2,700 to a token 270 soldiers.

The Security Council decision was greatly influenced by the resumption of open warfare between the RPF and the Rwandan army. RPF troops quartered in Kigali saw that UNAMIR would not act to protect civilians and feared that it would not execute its obligation to protect them either. On the day after the killing began, they left their barracks and engaged the Rwandan army soldiers in battle. The renewed hostilities complicated analysis of and reaction to the genocide. Careless and perhaps deliberately inaccurate reporting by the Secretary-General's special representative in Kigali, Jacques-Roger Booh Booh, convinced many Security Council members that the killings of civilians were just inter-ethnic violence, a spontaneous result of the resumption of the war. Only after the Security Council had voted to reduce the UNAMIR force did its members appear to realize that civilians were being slaughtered in a systematic fashion and often in areas remote from combat zones. Even after having realized the true nature of the genocide, they hesitated to act because they still hoped to be able to mediate the conflict. To take a strong position against the genocide could compromise the appearance of neutrality essential to serving as go-between in diplomatic negotiations between the two parties.

The Security Council was finally stung into action by continuing reports of massive slaughter and by the first enormous outpouring of refugees into Tanzania. After almost six weeks of genocide, the Security Council voted on May 17 to send back an enlarged UNAMIR force with a more extensive mandate, one that would allow it to defend civilians. But the political will to implement even this tardy action was lacking, and it took six months before the full UNAMIR force was in place.

With no effective action coming from outside the country and with the RPF tied up in battle with the regular Rwandan army, the perpetrators of genocide met no serious obstacles to expanding the slaughter. In those regions where local officials tried their best to resist, the central authorities removed and executed the resisters and sent in shock forces of militia and Presidential guard to push Hutu into killing their neighbors. In the southern prefecture of Butare, for example, the prefect Jean-Baptiste Habyalimana was removed on April 19 and executed soon after. "President" Sindikubwabo of the rump government went on the radio to demand that the people of Butare kill Tutsi "accomplices" in their area. That evening units of the Presidential Guard flew in from the capital and the massacres began almost immediately. One eyewitness recounted that on the night the guard arrived, they dug pits in the ground and filled them with burning tires. He saw people thrown live into the pits, including his sixty-year-old mother-in-law. Massive killings continued during the next days, and in the end thousands of Tutsi were slaughtered, virtually the entire Tutsi population of the region.

There was, of course, no way to hide violence on a genocidal scale, but authorities of the rump government tried at first to pass it off as "inter-ethnic fighting". As in earlier cases, they argued that the killings were a reaction—spontaneous and understandable—by Hutu in the face of massive Tutsi provocation: the assassination of Habyarimana and the resumption of the war by the RPF. In addition, they tried to justify the killings as essential to preempt a Tutsi plan to exterminate Hutu. The effort to disguise the genocide as "inter-ethnic" fighting succeeded temporarily, mostly because diplomats and foreign correspondents knew so little about Rwanda and fell into the explanation that seemed best to accord with their presumptions about Africa in general. But as groups like Human Rights Watch/Africa began to publish detailed analyses and as correspondents gathered more information on the spot, policymakers and the general public began to understand the real nature of the genocide.

The rump government persisted, however, in its efforts to disguise the crime. In September 1994, it circulated a pamphlet entitled "The Rwandan People

Accuses..." in which it said there had been a genocide during the preceding months, but that it had been a genocide of Hutu by the Tutsi, carried out with the cooperation of foreign powers like Belgium, the United States and the United Nations.

Accountability

The RPF defeated the rump government in mid-July and thus brought the genocide to an end. Long before the genocide was over, members of the United Nations began to talk about the need to punish the killers. An emergency meeting of the United Nations Human Rights Commission at the end of May appointed a special rapporteur to examine whether the slaughter was actually genocide. In his first report, the Special Rapporteur Rene Degni-Seguy concluded that genocide had been committed and that those guilty must be brought to justice. At the end of July, the Security Council established a commission of experts to give their assessment of the situation. In their reports, submitted in September and in November, they concurred in the finding of genocide and recommended that an international tribunal be established. The Security Council decided to enlarge the existing tribunal treating war crimes in the former Yugoslavia and to give it authority to prosecute persons accused of genocide, war crimes and crimes against humanity in Rwanda. The special prosecutor, Justice Richard Goldstone, has begun assembling evidence and expects to bring some cases to court in 1995.

The international tribunal will, however, deal with only a few dozen of the thousands of persons accused in the Rwandan tragedy. The new government of Rwanda will cooperate with the international tribunal in its prosecutions, but it has also announced its intention to bring all the other accused before its own courts. At first it lacked both the funds and the human resources to investigate and try the accused. During the genocide, many judges, prosecutors, and investigators died, fled or were themselves implicated in the killings. Soldiers of the RPA continued to arrest the accused even though there was no immediate prospect of their being tried or even formally charged with a crime. At the end of 1994 about 10,000 persons were being detained in overcrowded and inhumane conditions in official prisons. In addition, thousands of others were kept in even worse conditions in unofficial places of detention, such as military camps, private houses, latrines, and even shipping containers. The accused are arrested on the basis of denunciations, some of which are not justified. Innocent people have been accused particularly by those who seek to get hold of their property or to even the score from some prior conflict. The detention of persons against whom there is no credible presumption of guilt exacerbates bitterness and fear among Hutu. Beginning legitimate and orderly judicial procedures will help allay fears and defuse the bitternesss. The

Rwandan government has appealed for foreign judges and prosecutors to help try the accused. Such assistance has been promised and, if it materializes, will permit judicial procedures to begin quickly and to be carried out efficiently.

Prompt and effective prosecution of the accused would break with the pattern of impunity that has constituted an element common to all prior massacres. Punishing the guilty would demonstrate that ruthless exploitation of communal tensions, up to and including the level of genocide, is not an acceptable strategy for securing political power and would offer some hope of interrupting the cycle of violence.

RPF/RPA Abuses

In the course of their advance through Rwanda, RPF soldiers massacred groups of civilians—usually Hutu—in several communities. Many of these massacres took place in communities where large numbers of Tutsi had been killed during the genocide, and then were carried out with the encouragement and direction of Tutsi survivors. These killings diminished in number as the government extended its control, as UNAMIR troops were deployed, and as human rights monitors began establishing posts outside the capital.

Soldiers of the RPA have summarily executed persons arrested on accusations of genocide. Because no orderly records yet exist of the names of those detained in prisons or other sites, it is impossible to ascertain either the number or the identity of those who have been killed. The uncertainty about the fate of those taken away by the soldiers has led many Hutu to conclude, perhaps wrongly, that great numbers have been executed.

Some of those arrested by the RPA had recently returned either from refugee camps abroad or from displaced persons' camps elsewhere in Rwanda. News of their arrests has often spread back to the camps, fueling Hutu fears of returning home.

Because Tutsi civilians were often the ones to incite soldiers to execute, detain or otherwise abuse Hutu, many Hutu now see the RPA and the government they represent as operating only in the interest of Tutsi. And because many of those arrested or killed by the soldiers were notable people in their communities, some Hutu see these actions as part of a plan to eradicate all leaders among Hutu who might oppose the RPF.

Future Violence?

When the RPF defeated the former Rwandan government in mid-July 1994, they established a civilian government incorporating all the political parties provided for in the Arusha Accords with the exception of the MRND, which was clearly implicated in the genocide. Among the new civilian authorities, the president and the prime minister were both Hutu, as were the majority of cabinet ministers. Despite the presence of other parties and large numbers of Hutu leaders in the cabinet, the government was effectively directed by the RPF. With the RPF victory, the rump government and its army fled to Zaire, as did approximately one million refugees. Some of the refugees left because they feared reprisals from the advancing RPF troops. Others were forced to leave by the former government and its troops, who were determined that the RPF take over a country empty of people.

The arrival of the refugees in Zaire created an enormous crisis, to which the international community responded with prompt and generous humanitarian aid. Unable to distribute supplies by themselves, the aid agencies relied on the cooperation of the authorities of the rump government, particularly in the huge refugee camps in the Goma region of Zaire. These authorities then used their access to food, medicine and water to reinforce their control over the refugee community. They also siphoned off a percentage of the supplies for their own profit. In violation of the regulations of the United Nations High Commission for Refugees, members of the former Rwandan army and militia, still in uniform and many of them still armed, also received international aid. Not only were they directly nourished by the supplies, they were also enriched by what they stole from the more vulnerable parts of the refugee population, women, children and the elderly. Thus strengthened, the rump government and its army prepared a new attack on Rwanda, still motivated by a desire to defeat the RPF and to eliminate Tutsi from the country.

The rump government naturally wanted to keep the maximum number of people in the camps to validate their own claim to legitimacy and to prevent the resumption of normal life within Rwanda. They knew the international community was eager for the refugees to return home, and they intended to play upon this eagerness to win concessions from foreign powers and, through them, from the new Rwandan government. Using the still-operational RTLM radio, public meetings and word of mouth, officials of the rump government spread the story that Rwanda was virtually empty of people and that those Hutu who had not been killed had all fled.   They recounted stories of Hutu who had tried to return home only to be abused or killed by the RPF. Some of these accounts were, in fact, true, but many others were false or greatly exaggerated. When fear of the RPF was not enough to keep the refugees in the camps, they resorted to more direct intimidation or actual violence to keep them from taking the road back home. According to a Zairian human rights group monitoring the situation, one or two people are killed each day in the camps with no action taken against the killers.

Several hundred thousand people, many of them Hutu, remain in displaced persons' camps, especially in the southwestern part of Rwanda. As in the camps outside the country, former authorities have used control over humanitarian aid to rebuild their power. They discourage people from leaving the camps to return home and sometimes use force to keep them there. Gangs of the displaced use the camps as bases from which to launch raids to rob and kill local people. Some of this banditry may be purely criminal, but other instances are politically motivated efforts to destabilize local government control.

The new government decided to close the camps to impede the reorganization of militia and to halt the banditry. In early efforts to close the camps, RPA soldiers killed and wounded several persons. After international criticism, the government agreed to slow down the camp closings and to cooperate with U.N. officials to ensure greater security for the displaced as they were dispersed from the camps.

Regional Implications

Burundi, whose population of Hutu, Tutsi and Twa mirrors that of Rwanda, has experienced a different political history, in part because the Tutsi retained power after independence in 1962. Uprisings by Hutu to win control of the government have provoked savage reprisals by the Tutsi, notably in 1972 when perhaps one hundred thousand Hutu were killed. Although the countries have followed different paths, the hostilities between the groups are similar enough for violence in one country to provoke an immediate rise in tensions in the other. This echoing back and forth of violence is reinforced by the exchange of refugee populations, fearful and embittered, who flee with their anger into the adjacent country. Over the years, Rwandan Tutsi refugees have been among the most anti-Hutu people in Burundi and Hutu who have fled from Burundi have been among the most anti-Tutsi elements in Rwanda.

After political reforms in Burundi, a free and fair election in June 1993 put Melchior Ndadaye in the presidency. The first Hutu head of state in Burundi, he was betrayed by the army, which remained in the hands of the Tutsi. The soldiers led an abortive coup in October 1993 that assassinated Ndadaye and touched off communal violence that took approximately 50,000 lives, Hutu, Tutsi, and Twa. None of the killers involved in these massacres have been brought to trial or condemned and several persons accused of the assassination of Ndadaye remain in high civilian and military positions in the current government. The Tutsi extremism demonstrated by the coup raised the fears of Hutu within Rwanda, while impunity enjoyed by the killers encouraged them to procede with their own plans for massacring Tutsi. Once the genocide was launched, Burundi Hutu helped Rwandan Hutu slaughter Tutsi in such massacres as that at Cyahinda Parish in the

Butare prefecture. The subsequent RPF victory in Rwanda has heightened the desperation of Hutu within Burundi, who foresee a continuing Tutsi domination over the region as a whole. An underground Hutu movement is arming and training, in association with Hutu extremists from Rwanda now in camps in Zaire and Tanzania. A hate radio, modeled on RTLM, broadcasts incitements to violence in Burundi. Prompt prosecution of the accused in Rwanda may constitute one of the few hopes of halting the slide to greater violence in Burundi. Similarly, prosecutions within Burundi of those accused of killings in 1993 would also help to deter further slaughter.

Internal conditions in Zaire, too, have been gravely affected by the Rwandan genocide. Thousands of people of Rwandan origin—Hutu and Tutsi—lived in the North Kivu region of Zaire before the arrival of the current group of refugees. Some were descendants of people living in the region at the time colonial boundaries were drawn a century ago, others had migrated for economic reasons some sixty years ago, and still others had fled the violence in Rwanda during the 1960s. A year before the genocide began, there had been conflict between the people of Rwandan origin and other groups of the Zairian population, and approximately 7,000 people had been killed. The arrival of the large refugee population brought new tensions with the local peoples, especially when thousands of refugees left the camps and began filtering out into the adjacent communities, squatting on the land. In addition, soldiers and militia from among the refugees sometimes robbed and abused the local people. The Zairian soldiers sent supposedly to restore order in fact often made the situation worse because they also abused and stole from both the local population and the refugees. Until the refugees return to Rwanda, the whole of eastern Zaire will remain unstable with the likelihood of further violence between the various local and refugee groups.

Praising the Heroes

Despite enormous pressure—indeed sometimes at the cost of their own lives—many Hutu in Rwanda refused to participate in the slaughter. Countless Hutu went further and warned, hid, fed, transported, cared for and fought alongside Tutsi. Their heroism belies the simplistic notion spread by extremists that people of these two groups are bound to hate and kill one another.

INDIA

On December 6, 1992, the sixteenth-century Babur mosque in Ayodhya, Uttar Pradesh, was destroyed. During the preceding months, a movement of political parties, religious groups and cultural organizations, including the Bharatiya Janata Party (BJP), Rashtriya Swayamsevak Sangh (RSS), Vishwa Hindu Parishad (VHP) and Shiv Sena, called for the destruction of the mosque[1] as an integral move in their struggle for *Hindutva* or Hindu rule. Over 150,000 supporters known as *kar sevaks* converged on Ayodhya, where they attacked the three-domed mosque with hammers and pick-axes and reduced it to rubble. Despite the evident intent of the Hindutva ideologues and their supporters, the government of India did not attempt to stop the destruction of the mosque. Subsequently, kar sevaks rampaged through Ayodhya's Muslim neighborhoods, violently attacked Muslims, looted their shops, and set fire to their homes. Local police neither protected Ayodhya's Muslims nor sought to hold accountable those who perpetrated the violence.

In the following weeks, throughout India, Muslims publicly demonstrated against the events in Ayodhya. Initially, these demonstrations were stopped by the police. Later, protesting Muslims were attacked by Hindutva supporters. Large-scale communal riots between Muslims and Hindus ensued in which thousands of men, women, and children were killed and hundreds of women and girls were brutally raped by both sides. Moreover, tens of thousands were forcibly displaced as their homes and shops were destroyed. Many more fled out of fear of further violence. Muslims, who constitute twelve percent of India's population, suffered the worst abuses.

The government of India is complicit in the communal violence that occurred in the aftermath of Ayodhya, as the police not only failed to protect Muslims but also, in some areas such as Bombay, actively participated in the violence. The majority of those who organized or participated in communal violence, though readily identifiable, were not detained or prosecuted by either the police or local authorities. Furthermore, in the milieu of anti-Muslim violence, a number of Muslims were discriminatorily arrested under the provisions of the Terrorist and Disruptive Activities (Prevention) Act (TADA).

---

[1] Proponents of *Hindutva* claim that the site on which the Babur mosque was built is the birth place of the Hindu god Ram. Recorded disputes over the mosque, which was built in 1528, stem back to the nineteenth century. In 1949, after statues of Ram were placed in the mosque, the state government of Uttar Pradesh banned both Hindus and Muslims from entering the site under section 145 of the criminal penal code. The site continued to be under dispute when the mosque was razed.

The government of India appointed a number of commissions to investigate the destruction of the mosque in Ayodhya and the communal riots that followed. Thus far, no one has been held accountable for these events.[2] Moreover, a consistent pattern of violent discrimination against Muslims[3] continues to be widespread.

Background

Academic studies of communal conflicts in India have traditionally argued that religious antagonisms, particularly between Hindus and Muslims, are intrinsic to the region. The partition of British India into India and Pakistan is often cited as an example of the inevitability of conflict between religious groups in South Asia.[4] Such a simplified interpretation, however, is ahistoric and overlooks the complexity of relationships between India's numerous communities. It also fails to hold accountable political organizations and governments who have exploited religious differences for political purposes.

During the pre-colonial period, Hindus and Muslims did not define themselves in monolithic terms. Locality, caste, occupation, and language fractured notions of homogenous Hindu or Muslim communities. Furthermore, limitations in communications and transportation technologies inhibited the formation of India-wide communities. Thus, for example in Punjab, Hindu, Muslim, and Sikh landlords often formed powerful alliances against the local

---

[2] The government of India has on a number of occassions appointed commissions to investigate communal violence. In the majority of cases, the recommendations of the commissions have not been followed, nor have the guilty been held accountable. For example, in 1984, subsequent to the assassination of Indira Gandhi, 2,700 Sikhs were killed in anti-Sikh riots in Delhi. The police failed to protect Sikhs under attack and despite numerous commissions appointed to investigate this incident, over a decade later, no individuals have been prosecuted or punished for their involvement in this violent episode.

[3] While this report focuses on communal violence between Hindus and Muslims, throughout India members of lower castes and tribal groups (Dalits and Adivasis) are also consistently victims of violent human rights abuses in which the state is complicit.

[4] British India's partition, which saw the movement of Muslims to Pakistan and Hindus and Sikhs to India, involved the largest case of a population transfer along communal lines. An estimated seventeen million people migrated across across newly demarcated borders in a bloody movement which left three million dead.

peasantry. However, with the creation and expansion of a unitary state under the British, colonial authorities categorized India's various groups in monolithic terms through censuses[5] and other official records. Furthermore, the development of railroads and the vernacular press facilitated the dissemination of communal ideologies throughout the region.

In the late nineteenth century and early twentieth century, a strong pan-Indian anti-colonial movement emerged. The British, in an attempt to mollify nationalist organizations without conceding real political power, introduced a series of reforms which extended limited political rights to indigenous elites. In 1906, the British passed the Morley-Minto reforms which granted limited franchise. Under these reforms, Muslims voted in separate electorates from non-Muslims. Thus, Muslims across India had access to political power not as individual citizens but through a state-sanctioned Muslim leadership. Initially bound by locality, Hindus and Muslims needed to mobilize nationally along communal lines because representation by religious community was the key to political power.

The history of the subsequent years leading to independence in 1947 is contested, and analyses of the violence that accompanied partition vary dramatically.[6] Independent India established a governmental structure committed to secularism and democracy. Its constitution juridically guarantees equal treatment before the law to all individuals regardless of community background. The Congress Party, India's ruling party, consistently articulated its support for the equal recognition of all religions and communities. Despite state-sanctioned

---

[5] British census-makers classified Indians by monolithic religious categories. The religious classification system which was used to categorize Indians denied the possibility of multiple or changing identities. Many Indians, for example, practised rites and rituals of different faiths or particular to their region. Thus, for example, many Punjabis viewed themselves as members of local castes which were Hindu and Sikh or Hindu and Muslim. Moreover, the caste system which was fluid, was understood in colonial records as a static hierarchical structure. Thus, when caste affiliation was recorded, individuals were permanently locked into a social position which historically had shifted. Such classifications were used in the organization of the educational system, judiciary, army, and police. People were also governed by different personal religious laws, according to their ascribed religious community.

[6] Indian nationalist historiography attributed the division of India to the Muslim League, whereas Pakistani nationalist historiography points to the inflexibility of the Indian Nationalist Congress. Indian secular nationalists view the Congress as the representative body of Indian nationalism. Secularists also argue that contradictions within the Congress Party tarnish its reputation for nondiscrimination and secularism.

support for secularism and nondiscrimination, conservative religious organizations sought to give a communal orientation to political debates revolving around language issues, the protection of religious symbols, and the maintenance of religious personal laws. While the Congress Party often conceded to demands made by the religious right (in particular the Hindu right) over linguistic, religious, and legal issues, it remained legally and rhetorically committed to nondiscrimination and secularism in the political process.

A perceptible shift in the communalization of politics occurred during the 1970s when Indira Gandhi was prime minister. During this period, support for the Congress Party waned. Many of its post-independence development policies had failed, and massive inequities existed in access to education, housing, health care, and food. While India was procedurally a democracy, violations of human rights were widespread and endemic. Mrs. Gandhi increasingly resorted to authoritarian measures to retain power. She eventually declared a state of emergency in India and officially suspended a range of civil liberties. The suspension of regular government, which was followed by the defeat of the Congress Party and the election of the Janata Party in 1977, altered the Congress Party's traditionally leftist political platform.

The Congress Party was in disarray, and segments of its traditional base of support had shifted allegiance to other parties. It attempted to reconstitute itself by moving onto the ideological terrain traditionally occupied by right wing religious parties. For example, an effort to appeal to the Hindu right wing used Hindu rituals to inaugurate state functions and Hindu symbols were utilized at political rallies. Simultaneously, the Congress Party opportunistically sought support from conservative elements within the Muslim community while ignoring the sentiments of secular and progressive Muslims. Such strategies were politically successful, and the Congress was re-elected. After the assassination of Indira Gandhi in 1984, her successor and son, Rajiv Gandhi, continued the trend toward the communalization of politics. During the late 1980s and early 1990s the discriminatory rhetoric of an increasingly militant Hindu right was not condemned by the government. Rather, the government sought Hindutva electoral support and in 1984 Prime Minister Gandhi made a campaign speech from near Ayodhya, where he called for the rule of the Hindu god Ram over India. Similarly, attempts by conservative Muslims to assert power over the broader Indian Muslim community were supported by the government. For example, Gandhi promoted the agenda of conservative Muslim leaders who sought to uphold "traditional" Muslim family laws.

But despite the Congress Party's best efforts, it was the explicitly communal parties which benefited from the communalization of Indian politics.

In the 1989 national election, the BJP, with its explicit Hindutva agenda,[7] won 15 percent of the popular vote and eighty-eight seats in Parliament. In addition, it gained control of four state assemblies including Uttar Pradesh. The BJP had campaigned on a Hindutva platform which promised, among other things, to build a temple dedicated to Ram on the site of the Babur mosque in Ayodhya.

Ayodhya

Hindutva ideologues have argued that the site on which the Babur mosque was built is the birthplace of Ram and in order to achieve *Ram Rajya* (the rule of Ram) in India, a temple needed to be constructed there. Disputes over the contested site started in 1885 when a court case was filed to build a temple in the mosque's outer courtyard. The case was rejected. In 1949, Ram idols were illegally installed in the mosque. While Prime Minister Nehru called for the removal of the idols, the courts declared that neither Hindus nor Muslims were allowed to enter the building. The idols remained, and Muslims lost the right to worship in the mosque. Until the mid-1980s, disputes over the structure involved local Muslims and Hindus and the courts. In 1984, the VHP demanded the site be handed over to Hindus, and a committee was formed to acheive this goal. The courts refused to make a decision as to the ownership of the structure. The VHP campaigned vigorously for the construction of a temple and expanded the movement from Ayodhya to all of India, creating and exacerbating communal tensions from Gujarat to Karnataka. In 1987, the state government of Uttar Pradesh transferred the cases connected with the mosque from the district court to the high court. In 1989, the high court transferred the cases to a specially designated three-judge court. Cases eventually moved to the Supreme Court, where no decisions over use of the structure were made.

In November 1989, the state government allowed the performance of Hindu rituals at the disputed site. In June 1991, in state elections, the BJP took power in Uttar Pradesh. Having pledged to build the temple, the state government sought to achieve that goal. Supporters for the destruction of the mosque were systematically mobilized by Hindutva organizations through public speeches, the print media, and on audio and video cassettes distributed by local branches of these organizations. Kar sevaks were urged to travel to Ayodhya to build a temple on the

---

[7] BJP ideologues argue that as the essence of democracy is majority rule, and because Hindus constitute the majority of Indians, India must be governed by the principles of Hinduism. Such an argument however, is based on the flawed premise that democracy is the same as majoritarianism and that the majority of Indians subscribe to a monolithic interpretation of Hinduism.

site of the mosque. In November 1992, Hindus from all over India began to assemble at Ayodhya with the stated intent of destroying the mosque. Some 27,000 had arrived before November 29, 50,000 by December 1, 90,000 on December 2, and 150,000 the following day. Acts of communal violence began on December 1, when kar sevaks started vandalizing Muslim graveyards. The local administration allowed kar sevaks to converge on Ayodhya but stopped peace marches by groups who opposed their agenda. On December 5, religious leaders declared that a new temple dedicated to Ram would be constructed at noon the next day. On December 6, in a series of vitriolic anti-Muslim speeches, political and religious leaders, including L.K. Advani, the leader of the BJP and a member of Parliament, provoked their supporters to destroy the mosque and begin construction of a temple. As a result, in a seven-hour frenzy, over 100,000 kar sevaks demolished the mosque with hammers, pick-axes, and crowbars and began to clear the rubble to erect a canopy to house idols of Ram.

In the aftermath of the destruction, Ayodhya's Muslim community was systematically attacked by Hindu mobs for two days. Fourteen Muslims were killed and 267 houses, twenty-three mosques, and nineteen grave sites were destroyed. The local, state, and central governments clearly chose to permit the destruction of the mosque and in fact, helped facilitate the activities of the kar sevaks. In the weeks leading up to December 6, the issue of the protection of the mosque was discussed widely in governmental institutions including the national parliament, the Uttar Pradesh legislature, the Supreme Court, and the Uttar Pradesh High Court in Allahabad. Despite more than adequate warnings that the mosque would be destroyed and Muslims in the region would be victims of communal violence, state and local security forces around the mosque were actually reduced in early December. The Police Armed Constabulary (PAC), a security force known for its communal bias, was deployed in Ayodhya by the state government, ensuring that the destruction of the mosque would meet little resistance. The central government failed to deploy any force whatsoever in the area. After the mosque was destroyed, Uttar Pradesh state security forces were directly involved in attacks against Muslims. From December 7 onwards, the departure of tens of thousands of kar sevaks was facilitated by the provision of special trains organized by Hindutva organizations with the full knowledge of the Uttar Pradesh government. No effort was made to identify or detain those involved in the violence, even though the attacks took place in clear sight of state security forces.

The Bombay Riots

Images of the destruction of the mosque at Ayodhya were disseminated throughout India on BBC television. Muslims and advocates for a secular India publicly demonstrated their outrage at the failure of the state to intervene effectively. Such demonstrations consistently met an abusive response from the police and Hindutva organizations. In various centers throughout India, including Delhi, Hyderabad, Bijapur, Calcutta, Surat, and Ahmedabad, communal violence ensued in which thousands were killed. In particular, post-Ayodhya communal violence wrought widespread destruction in Bombay, India's cosmopolitan commercial center and state capital of Maharashtra.

During the week following the events in Ayodhya, Muslims held public demonstrations in the streets of Bombay, targeted not against Hindus, but against the government which had failed to prevent the destruction of the mosque. Many of these spontaneous gatherings, particularly in south and central Bombay, degenerated into violent attacks against police officers. Government property, including public transport facilities and police stations, was also attacked. The police, who responded quickly and efficiently, sought to quash both the violent attacks and the peaceful demonstrations. Rather than shouting warnings to the crowds to disperse, or using tear gas or non-lethal weapons, the police opened fire on the crowds. Guns were not directed to the feet or above the crowds but rather directly at areas of the body which could suffer fatal injuries. The majority of those killed were Muslims who died of bullet wounds to the head or chest. Direct fire by the police was systematically employed in over fifteen police jurisdictions in Bombay, clearly indicating that the various police stations were acting on orders from a senior city-wide level. Bombay's Police Commissioner, Srikant Bapat, asserted that the use of firepower by the police was "deliberate, controlled, and effective" to "prevent two communities from clashing."

For the ten days following December 6, much of the violence took place between the police and Muslims. In addition to firing on demonstrators, police entered Muslim households, conducted arbitrary arrests, tortured those arrested, burned down homes, and fired on defenseless residents. During the same period, Hindus, who formed processions supporting the destruction of the mosque, were not stopped by the police. In the latter days of the violence, members of the Shiv Sena, a Maharashtrian political organization with a Hindutva agenda, began to attack Muslim households alongside the police.

Official figures estimate that 167 people were killed between December 6 and 16. Individuals interviewed by Human Rights Watch/Asia, however, indicate that these statistics were grossly understated. Nongovernmental organizations in Bombay claimed that approximately 500 were killed. As a large number of residents fled Bombay, such statistics are extremely difficult to verify.

Between December 17, 1992 and January 4, 1993 the city was relatively quiet, although many areas were tense and there were individual incidents of stabbing and arson. The violence, however, was not on the scale witnessed in the week following the mosque's destruction. In late December and early January the Shiv Sena led Hindu religious processions throughout Bombay. On January 5, 1992 two union workers were killed in an ordinary labor dispute. However, in an atmosphere suffused with communal tensions, these killings were cast in communal terms, and on January 6, violence in Bombay re-emerged with clashes between Hindus and Muslims in central Bombay, Dharavi, Mahim, and Masjid. In January 1992, much of the violence was directed by members of the Shiv Sena who stopped cars, identified Muslim passengers, and attacked them.[8] Members of the Shiv Sena (*Shiv Sainiks*) systematically attacked Muslim men, women, and children in their homes and on the streets, set their residences and shops on fire and in many instances brutally murdered them. In addition, many Muslim women were raped. Publicly brandishing weaponry including swords, metal bars, and batons, Shiv Sainiks and other anti-Muslim Hindus attacked Muslims across the city. The riots in January spread to regions traditionally not prone to communal violence, including some of Bombay's most affluent localities.   Many Shiv Sainiks had municipal lists which named shopowners and electoral rolls which identified residents of specific homes, thus they were able to identify Muslim property which was systematically destroyed. While there was violence against Hindus as well, the overwhelming majority of the more than 1,000 individuals killed in Bombay in January were Muslims. As Muslim stores, restaurants, and service centers were destroyed tens of thousands fled to refugee camps and to areas surrounding Bombay. In at least three instances in January 1993, unions controlled by the Shiv Sena forced employers at major businesses, such as the Oberoi Hotels, to dismiss Muslim employees. In stark juxtaposition to police retaliation against Muslims in the preceding month, the police did not get involved in the initial days of the January riots and consistently failed to protect Muslims. In fact, transcripts of police radio conversations, obtained by journalists and shown to Human Rights Watch, reveal an explicit disregard for Muslim safety. In one recording the Bombay Police Control Room told a mobile police unit: "Don't burn anything belonging to a Maharashtrian. But burn everything belonging to a Muslim."

Journalists and newspaper editors who vocally opposed the Shiv Sena or the Hindutva agenda, whether or not they were Muslim, were also victims of violence. Journalists from Bombay vernacular papers including *Urdu Blitz, Urdu Times, Inquilab,* and *Mahanagar* were threatened with violence and/or physically attacked. The Shiv Sena paper *Saamna* actively disseminated anti-Muslim

---

[8]As Hindus and Muslims share common physical traits mobs often pulled down the pants of men to see if they were circumcised and thus ostensibly Muslim.

propaganda and called on patriotic Indians to rid the country of foreign terrorists, who were, they claimed, predominantly Muslim.

Justice B.N. Srikrishnan of the Bombay High Court was called upon by the government to perform an inquiry into the violence that ravaged Bombay in December 1992 and January 1993. He was to submit his report within six months. The commission received thousands of affadavits and interviewed hundreds of victims and witnesses. However, as of February 1995 it had failed to hold anyone responsible for perpetrating acts of communal violence or to produce any report. By contrast, within three months of the riots, two retired judges of the Bombay High Court, Justices S.M. Daud and H. Suresh, conducted an independent inquiry which was published by the nongovernmental Indian Human Rights Commission.[9] This inquiry explicitly indicts individuals from the state government, the police, and the Shiv Sena for their role in Bombay's communal violence. The report by Daud and Suresh summarizes evidence which illustrates violations of human rights committed by the police against Muslims. It provides for example, a list of eighty-one police officers including a former joint commissioner and a deputy commissioner who were named by witnesses for their direct role in the riots. Of the eighty-one police officers, thirty-five were inspectors, twenty-four sub-inspectors, and twelve constables. Additionally the report cites over 700 people in twenty-six localities alleged to be involved in the riots, including political leaders from the Shiv Sena, Congress Party, and the BJP. This report shows that if the government was genuinely concerned with upholding its legal obligations *vis à vis* the protection of minority rights, it could draw on a large body of evidence to substantiate cases and initiate prosecution. However, according to *Communalism Combat*, a Bombay-based newspaper established by a prominent journalist, of the 2,278 cases filed with the police for activities relating to communal violence in Bombay between December 1992 and January 1993, by June 1994, 848 of the accused had cases filed against them, 1,333 cases were closed for lack of evidence, ninety-seven cases were ongoing, and no trials had begun.[10]

The impunity enjoyed by those explicitly involved in acts of communal violence was illustrated by the failure of the state to charge Bal Thackeray, the

---

[9] S.M. Daud and H. Suresh, *The People's Verdict* (Bombay: Indian Human Rights Commission, 1993.)

[10] *Communalism Combat* (Bombay), "Call for Public Meeting to Demand Action from the State Government and the Police Against those Guilty for Inciting and Participating in theViolence of December 1992 and January 1993 in Bombay," June 10, 1994.

leader of the Shiv Sena, despite the considerable body of evidence available to establish a case against him. The state's failure to hold individual Shiv Sainiks accountable for their actions follows a consistent pattern of state failure to hold the Shiv Sena more generally accountable for its role in communal violence. In the 1960s and 1970s, it helped the Congress government to crush Communist Party-led trade unions through organized violence. For its support in busting the unions, the Shiv Sena was granted virtual immunity from prosecution. In 1970, it was involved in communal riots in Bhiwandi that left one hundred dead. The state appointed the Madon Commission, which indicted the Shiv Sena and the police for the riots, but no action was taken against the Shiv Sena. In 1984, the Shiv Sena was again involved in riots in Bhiwandi which according to official figures left 278 dead and 1,115 injured, the majority of whom were Muslim. Again, no Shiv Sena member was prosecuted or punished.

TADA, Communal Violence, and the Bomb Blasts
        On March 12, 1992, Bombay was shaken by a series of bomb blasts which killed 357 people and injured 700. Twelve bombs exploded in a variety of places including the Bombay Stock Exchange, the Air India Office, and three hotels. A criminal investigation conducted by the Bombay police with support from the Central Bureau of Investigation, the Central Forensic Science Laboratory, the army, and Interpol, began immediately. Two Muslims based in Dubai known as the Memon brothers were accused as the primary perpetrators. The police portrayed the bomb blasts as a Muslim attack against the city, directed by the Pakistan government. Over 400 predominantly Muslim residents of Behrampada, Mahim, Byculla, and Nagpada were immediately detained for alleged involvement in the bombings, one hundred of whom were eventually charged under the anti-terrorist law known as TADA, together with sixty-five who were arrested later.
        In stark contrast to their laxity in investigating the perpetrators of communal violence, the police vigorously sought to arrest and punish those allegedly responsible for the bomb blasts and offered rewards totalling US$4.8 million for information leading to the arrest of suspects wanted in connection with the blasts. Within seven months of the blasts the police completed their investigation, collected testimony from 3,741 witnesses, and filed a 9,392-page charge sheet. In addition to the TADA charges, defendants were accused of murder, attempted murder, causing hurt and grievous harm, and mischief under the Indian Criminal Code, as well as violations of the Arms Act, the Explosives Act, and the Prevention of Damage to Public Property Act. For the Muslims of Bombay, the state's willingness to prosecute those involved in the bomb blasts while failing to hold perpetrators of earlier anti-Muslim communal violence

accountable, reinforced a loss of faith in the state and its ability to protect them.

The arrests pointed to the more general problem of the tendency to use TADA in a discriminatory fashion. Introduced as a temporary measure in 1985 to stop terrorist acts, it seeks to punish a vaguely defined range of activities defined as disruptive.[11] Those charged under the act can be held without being produced before a magistrate for up to one year. Confessions made before police offciers are admissable as evidence, the identity of witnesses can be kept secret, designated courts can prosecute TADA detainees *in camera*, and the onus of proof is shifted on to the accused. The provisions of the act allow for unchecked discrimination by the police and the judiciary. In communally sensitive contexts such as Bombay, the law has been used to target religious minorities. Muslims have also been targeted by TADA in other parts of India. In particular, the state of Gujarat, where there have been over 15,000 TADA arrests since 1985, has used the law against Muslims in communal riots.[12]

Conclusion

Communal violence in India has reached unprecedented levels in the 1990s. Where conflicts were once localized, they now occur on a national scale. At the level of rhetoric, the government claims to be committed to secularism and nondiscrimination. However, there is a conspicuous tendency by the government to ignore the scale of violence and human suffering during communal violence. Laxity in enforcing the law and the failure to punish those involved sends the wrong signals to both law-breakers and law enforcers across the country. The government of India is proud of its claim to be a democracy with a strong commitment to the rule of law. India's constitution and legal system juridically guarantee the protection of basic human rights to its citizens, including the right to protection of the law, the right to due process, and the right to equal treatment before the law regardless of religion, caste, or class. Under customary international law, India is obligated to guarantee human rights set forth and defined in the

---

[11] Under TADA, a disruptive activity is defined as "any action taken, whether by act or speech or through any other media or in any manner whatsoever: (i) which questions, disrupts, or is intended to disrupt, whether directly or indirectly, the sovereignty and territorial integrity of India; or (ii) which is intended to bring about or supports any claim, whether directly or indirectly, for the secession of any part of India from the Union."

[12] People's Union for Democratic Rights, *Lawless Roads, A Report on TADA 1985-1993* (Delhi, 1993), pp. 37-40.

International Covenant of Civil and Political Rights. However, the denial of justice to victims of communal violence reveals a divergence between India's legal obligations and the practices of its police, judiciary, and officials at various levels of government.

ISRAELI-OCCUPIED TERRITORIES

The violent conflict described in this chapter is unique in many respects. It takes place on land that is recognized by the international community as being under Israeli military occupation. The two populations in conflict are the nearly two million Palestinian Muslim and Christian residents of the West Bank and Gaza Strip, regarded as "protected persons" by humanitarian law, and the 300,000 Jews, almost all of them Israeli citizens, who have settled in these two areas, both occupied by Israel since 1967.[1]

The Jewish settlements are illegal under the applicable international law. Article 49.6 of the Fourth Geneva Convention states, in part, "The Occupying Power shall not deport or transfer parts of its own civilian population into the territory it occupies." Through land confiscations, subsidies, low-interest mortgages, generous infrastructural spending and other measures, the government of Israel has since 1967 actively facilitated and promoted the transfer of Jews from Israel (and Jewish immigrants arriving from abroad) into the West Bank and Gaza Strip.[2]

Relations between the settler and the Palestinian population have been marked by simmering tension and outbursts of violence. In general, Palestinians view settlers as usurping Palestinian land and resources, and as a threat to the safety and well-being, if not the very survival, of the Palestinian community on what it considers as its land. Many, if not most Jewish settlers believe that they have an equal if not superior claim to the land and resources of the West Bank and Gaza Strip, and in turn feel physically threatened by Palestinian activists, ranging from

---

[1] These figures include the 162,000 Jews and 155,000 Palestinians who live in East Jerusalem, which Israel unilaterally annexed in 1967. This annexation has not been recognized by the international community, which considers East Jerusalem to be occupied territory, like the rest of the West Bank. The pattern of violence described in this report, however, occurs primarily in the West Bank, excluding East Jerusalem.

The study does not concern relations between Jews and Palestinian Arabs who reside inside the state of Israel, where serious incidents of communal violence are infrequent.

[2] See Geoffrey Aronson, *Israel, Palestinians and the Intifada: Creating Facts in the West Bank* (London: Kegan Paul International, 1990). The International Committee of the Red Cross, generally considered to be the guardian of the Geneva Conventions, contends that the implantation of settlements in the occupied territories, "carried out with the Israeli authorities' support, constitutes a violation of the Fourth Convention, in particular Articles 27, 47 and 49." *Annual Report 1983* (Geneva: ICRC, 1984), p. 67.

throwers of stones and molotov cocktails to armed militants. Settlers are permitted to carry weapons and routinely do so outside their settlements, while Palestinian civilians are forbidden to bear arms.

The proximity in which settlers and Palestinians live has kept tensions simmering. Members of both communities have targeted members of the other for violent assaults. Incidents have included stone-throwing, vandalism, arson, firebombing, and armed attacks. Scores of persons on both sides have been killed, hundreds have been wounded, and property damage has been extensive.[3] Human Rights Watch vigorously condemns deliberate attacks against any civilians, whether carried out by security forces, insurgent organizations, or civilian groups of any nationality. Whether the victims are Israelis or Palestinians, such attacks violate one of the most fundamental norms of humanitarian law.

The Israeli-Palestinian peace process has not significantly altered the overall situation described in this chapter. Despite the transfer to a Palestinian authority of some powers over most of the Gaza Strip and the town of Jericho, and lesser powers over the rest of the West Bank, settler- Palestinian violence has continued. The area in which the vast majority of incidents occurred, the West Bank, remains under direct Israeli occupation, except for the tiny enclave of Jericho. The peace process has in fact heightened tensions over settlements and Palestinian-settler violence, with both Israelis and Palestinians facing the prospect of negotiating the disposition of land and settlements, pursuant to the Declaration of Principles signed by the government of Israel and the Palestine Liberation Organization in September 1993.[4]

As the occupying power, the Israeli military government has a duty to investigate and prosecute criminal offenses. But in contrast to the vigorous and often brutal methods that the government has employed when responding to attacks on Israelis by militant Palestinians, settler violence has been met by laxness on the

---

[3] In incidents that occurred inside the occupied territories, Palestinians have killed seventy-two Israeli civilians and two tourists, and Israeli civilians have killed one hundred Palestinians between December 1987, when the Palestinian uprising, or intifada, began, and the end of February 1995. Settlers account for most of the Israeli victims and perpetrators in these fatal incidents. The figure is provided by B'Tselem, the Israeli Information Center for Human Rights in the Occupied Territories.

[4] These issues are among those to be deferred until "permanent-status negotiations," according to Article Five of the Declaration of Principles. Such negotiations are to commence no later than the beginning of the third year of the five-year "interim period," i.e., by May 1996.

part of the security forces and leniency by the court system. Soldiers of the Israel Defense Forces (IDF), the main body responsible for law enforcement in the territories, stand by while settlers engage in acts of violence against Palestinians and their property, and in some instances soldiers have joined settlers in the violence. The Israel Police, the agency with primary responsibility for the criminal investigation of offenses committed by settlers, investigates these offenses inadequately if at all. Settlers are rarely brought to trial for violent offenses against Palestinians, and those convicted almost invariably receive light sentences. This double standard has made the government complicit in settler violence, by giving its perpetrators a sense of virtual impunity for their illegal actions. It also is a vivid example of the failure of the government of Israel to fulfil its humanitarian obligations to protect the population under occupation.[5]

After exposing a double standard in how the security forces in the West Bank had responded to acts of violence by Palestinians and settlers, the official commission of inquiry into the Hebron massacre (known as the "Shamgar Commission") suggested a wholly appropriate standard that, if attained, would go a long way toward protecting Palestinians from settler violence:

> The law must be enforced with rigor, decisiveness and equality, against anyone who breaks it, and no one can excuse his actions with the fact that another crime has been committed and that its perpetrator was not caught nor prosecuted.[6]

This chapter documents how far Israeli official conduct has been from this principle. But in criticizing the Israeli double standard in enforcing the law and administering justice, Human Rights Watch does not wish to suggest that Israel's settlement policy would somehow be less illegal if the government enforced laws and administered justice toward Palestinians and Jews in a manner that was entirely

---

[5] An occupying power is responsible for the well-being of residents of the occupied territories, including protection from acts of violence. Article 43 of the Hague Regulations of 1907 require the occupying power to "take all measures...to restore, and ensure, as far as possible, public order and safety..." Article 27 of the Fourth Geneva Convention requires that "protected persons ... shall be protected especially against all acts of violence or threats thereof."

[6] *Commission of Inquiry into the Massacre at the Tomb of the Patriarchs in Hebron: Excerpts from the Report* (Jerusalem: Government Press Office, June 1994), p. 24.

non-discriminatory.

Background

In the late 19th century, the population of Palestine, which was part of the Ottoman Empire, was approximately half a million people, of whom a majority were Muslims, about sixteen percent Christians and five percent Jews. Beginning in the 1880s Eastern European Jews began to immigrate to Palestine in large numbers. Between 1882 and 1914, the Jewish population increased from 24,000 to 85,000.[7] After the collapse of the Ottoman Empire in the First World War, the League of Nations entrusted Britain with a mandate over Palestine. Jewish immigration continued under British rule, despite the increasingly vocal opposition of the local Arab population.

In 1947, Great Britain informed the United Nations it wished to terminate its mandate. The U.N. General Assembly passed Resolution 181, calling for the partition of Palestine into a Jewish and an Arab state. Arab leaders rejected this partition. In 1948, on the eve of the British withdrawal, Israel declared its independence, and in the war that followed, Israel gained control of all mandatory Palestine except for the Gaza Strip and what is today called the West Bank (including the eastern part of Jerusalem). Jordan annexed and administered the West Bank, and Egypt administered the Gaza Strip. In the 1967 war, Israel occupied both of these territories.

In the years following the 1967 war, the Israeli government, led by the Labor Party, embarked on the large-scale construction of Jewish neighborhoods in East Jerusalem, which it had unilaterally annexed. The government also built several settlements in the West Bank, mostly in the sparsely populated eastern flank, near the border with Jordan. Settlements nearer to Palestinian population centers were also erected in this period by movements such as *Gush Emunim* (the Bloc of the Faithful), which claim the West Bank as integral parts of the "Greater Land of Israel" to which Jews are entitled by divine mandate. A crucial precedent in the settlement movement came in April 1968, when several Israeli families occupied a Hebron hotel and two buildings near the military governorate of the Hebron area. They remained in Hebron for six months until the Israeli government acquiesced to their demands to establish a settlement near Hebron. Many early Israeli settlements followed this pattern: an illegal encampment that initially met with government ambivalence and later with government support.

The hesitation of authorities toward settlement expansion ended when the

---

[7] Neville J. Mandel, *The Arabs and Zionism Before World War I* (Berkeley: University of California Press, 1976).

Likud party came to power in 1977 and accelerated settlement growth, including in the central West Bank areas densely populated by Palestinians, in order to solidify Israel's claims on the West Bank. Since then, successive Labor- and Likud-led governments have provided generous incentives, including financial subsidies, security protection, and infrastructural improvements, to encourage Israelis to settle in the occupied territories. By the end of 1994, 293,000 Israelis lived in the West Bank, including 162,000 in East Jerusalem, and 4,000 lived in the Gaza Strip.[8]

Until 1979, the most commonly used grounds on which land was acquired for the construction of settlements were: requisition for military purposes, seizure of (Jordanian or Egyptian) government property, and expropriation for public purposes. Following an Israeli High Court ruling that private property could not be confiscated for Israeli settlement,[9] the government resorted to a practice of classifying "uncultivated" or "unregistered" property as "state land" and thereby making it susceptible to confiscation and then allocation to settlers. By the mid-1980s, Israel had established control over almost fifty percent of the land in the West Bank and forty percent of the Gaza Strip.[10]

The Role of the Government of Israel

While some settlements were initially established in defiance of Israeli law and many militant settlers view the government as hostile to their objectives, settlements are state-sanctioned communities. Israel provides its citizens living in the territories with all of the public services provided inside Israel. State policies of water allocation, taxation, land ownership, building permits, and infrastructure development favor Israeli settlers and discriminate against Palestinians.

In order to protect settlements, the government has invested in their security infrastructure, as well as maintaining arms stockpiles and communications and paramilitary equipment at settlements. IDF units and settlers collaborate in patrol activities. Each settlement has a security coordinator responsible for liaison with regional military commanders. At night, soldiers are frequently posted within

---

[8] Foundation for Middle East Peace, *Report on Israeli Settlement in the Occupied Territories,* vol. 5, no. 1, January 1995, p. 4.

[9] *Dweikat v. Government of Israel* (the "Elon Moreh" case), HCJ 390/79.

[10] Meron Benvenisti, *West Bank Data Base Project Report 1986* (Jerusalem: The Jerusalem Post, 1986), pp. 25-26; and Meron Benvenisti, "The Hill of Strife," *Haaretz,* December 29, 1994.

and around settlements, and military patrols are routinely assigned to guard convoys of settlers as they travel in the territories.

Like other Israeli Jews, settlers are conscripted into the military. They are in active service for three years and then serve in the reserves until the age of fifty-five. Settlers may receive permission to keep their army-issued weapons all year round, as well as obtain licenses for hand guns. Under District Defense Regulations, settlers may perform their reserve service in their areas of residence. Even notorious settler extremists have performed their reserve service in the territories. The late Meir Kahane, founder of the Kach party, which favors the forcible expulsion of Palestinians from the West Bank, was assigned to perform reserve service in the Palestinian city of Ramallah in 1982 despite a court order forbidding his entry into the city.[11]

Different legal systems apply to Palestinian and Israeli residents of the territories. The law in force in the West Bank (excluding annexed East Jerusalem) consists of a combination of the British Defense (Emergency) Regulations of 1945, Jordanian law and Israeli military orders.[12] Both Jordanian civil courts and Israeli military courts function in the West Bank. A 1967 military order empowered military courts to adjudicate all criminal offenses recognized by the Israeli authorities, whether under previously enacted law or under the military government's own legislation.[13] Since the outbreak of the intifada, nearly all Palestinian defendants have been tried in military courts.

In theory, Israelis in the occupied territories are subject to the same legal regime. However, a 1967 military order makes them subject to Israeli criminal law as well. The jurisdictional conflict is resolved by a policy of applying Israeli law

---

[11] Foundation for Middle East Peace, *Report on Israeli Settlement in the Occupied Territories*, Vol. 4, No. 3, (Washington, D.C., May 1994), p. 4.

[12] Annexed East Jerusalem is subject to the laws in force in the state of Israel. In the Gaza Strip, a mixture of Egyptian and Ottoman laws, British Defense Emergency Regulations, and Israel military orders have been in force since 1967. In May 1994, limited powers of self-rule over much of Gaza Strip were transferred to a Palestinian Authority, pursuant to agreements reached between the government of Israel and the Palestine Liberation Organization.

[13] Col. David Yahav, ed., *Israel, the "Intifada" and the Rule of Law* (Tel Aviv: Ministry of Defense Publications, 1993), p.86.

to Israeli citizens and non-Israeli Jews in the territories.[14]   By virtue of this policy, persons living side-by-side are subject to different legal systems according to their national identity.

The dual system discriminates in favor of settlers and against Palestinians. For example, Palestinian suspects can be held without charge for eighteen days before they must be brought before a judge; an Israeli detainee, held under Israeli law, must be brought before a judge within forty-eight hours. Palestinian suspects are usually interrogated by the IDF or the General Security Service (the "Shabak", or "Shin Bet"), both of which engage in a systematic pattern of ill-treatment and torture of Palestinian detainees.[15]   Israeli suspects are, with rare exception,[16] investigated by the Israel Police. Their treatment while under interrogation is not nearly as harsh as that meted out to Palestinians, although complaints are sometimes lodged. A conviction for manslaughter in the military court carries a maximum sentence of life imprisonment; a conviction for the same offense in an Israeli civil court carries a maximum sentence of twenty years imprisonment.

For the purported aim of preventing anti-Israel violence, the government also applies a wide range of measures against Palestinians, including mass detentions and collective punishments such as curfews and area closures. Without endorsing them, it is worth pointing out that none of these measures are ever used against settlers in order to deter violent behavior on their part.

In sum, the government of Israel has, in defiance of international law, encouraged and assisted in the establishment of well-armed Jewish enclaves near to, and often on land seized from, Palestinians. The government has provided settlers with resources and rights that are vastly superior to those enjoyed by the Palestinians, and has been lax in investigating and punishing offenses committed by settlers against Palestinians.

---

[14] An exception is the use of the Defense (Emergency) Regulations in effect in the West Bank to administratively detain five settler militants from the Kach and Kahane Chai organizations following the Hebron massacre. See below.

[15] Human Rights Watch/Middle East, *Torture and Ill-treatment: Israel's Interrogation of Palestinians from the Occupied Territories* (New York: Human Rights Watch, 1994).

[16] In the autumn of 1994, several West Bank settlers accused of involvement in an organization plotting to kill Palestinians were interrogated by the GSS.

Acts of Settler Violence

Palestinian human rights organizations that have documented settler violence against their communities since the late 1970's point to two main patterns of settler violence. The first is the use of excessive force during confrontations with Palestinians. This includes shooting wildly or with intent to kill in response to non-life-threatening stone-throwing or to roadblocks. According to a study conducted by B'Tselem, Israeli civilians killed sixty-two Palestinians in the territories between 1988 and 1993. In at least forty-nine cases, the Israelis were in no imminent danger. In only seven cases did Israelis open fire in response to life-threatening situations, and in three of these cases the Israelis had knowingly put themselves in danger.[17]

Another pattern of settler violence consists of organized attacks by armed settlers moving through Arab communities, vandalizing property, intimidating and provoking confrontations with local inhabitants. Vigilante raids of this type frequently take place in the wake of attacks on settlers by Palestinian militants, and are arbitrary and indiscriminate: the identity or residence of the perpetrator is usually not yet known to the settlers. Sometimes, raids are not provoked by a specific deed, but intended rather to "demonstrate a presence" or facilitate land confiscation efforts. The well-organized and consistent character of many of these operations suggests that some are planned and coordinated.

Settlers also have been involved in the abduction of Palestinian youths. During the first eighteen months of the intifada, the Jerusalem-based Palestine Human Rights Information Center reported twenty-one cases in which Palestinians, most of them boys under the age of fifteen, were seized by settlers, beaten and then either released in a remote area or turned over to authorities.[18] One settler explained: "We do not kidnap people, but sometimes we grab a kid for throwing stones and take him to the settlement, rough him up a little, and then hand him over

---

[17] B'Tselem, *Law Enforcement vis-à-vis Israeli Civilians in the Occupied Territories* (Jerusalem: B'Tselem, 1994). (This report is in Hebrew; an English-language summary was issued in March 1994; the full English-language text is in press). In the remaining six cases, B'Tselem said it had insufficient information to determine whether the use of lethal force was justified.

[18] The Database Project on Palestinian Human Rights, *Colonial Pursuits: Settler Violence during the Uprising in the Occupied Territories* (Chicago: Database Project on Palestinian Human Rights, 1989), pp. 21-22.

to the army so that they can finish the job."[19] But while settlers may claim they are carrying out citizen arrests of offenders, human rights organizations have documented cases where children were abducted at random.

Israel Defense Forces

The IDF has ultimate responsibility for the safety of all residents of the territories. However, its jurisdiction over Israeli settlers is unclear. The Shamgar Commission, investigating the Hebron Massacre, revealed contradictions between stated IDF policy, orders communicated to soldiers, and soldiers' understanding of their instructions. For example, while high-ranking IDF officials have stated that soldiers are responsible for arresting settlers and turning them over to the police for investigation, soldiers in the field have consistently reported that they are forbidden from arresting settlers except in the most extreme circumstances.

In December 1993, the army published a booklet entitled *Procedures for Enforcing Law and Order vis-à-vis Israeli Residents of the Territories*. The booklet states IDF soldiers are authorized to arrest settlers. However, testimony taken from reserve soldiers by B'Tselem a month after this booklet's distribution revealed that officers were still instructing soldiers not to arrest settlers.[20]

The confusion over interpreting policy is further illustrated by open-fire regulations in situations involving settlers. The IDF procedures booklet for settlers states in underlined text, "it will be emphasized that soldiers are not to use weapons against an Israeli."[21] In testimony provided to the Shamgar Commission, Gen. Shaul Mofaz, commander of military forces in the West Bank, confirmed that soldiers were forbidden from shooting at Jews, though he denied its applicability to situations akin to massacre.[22] General Mofaz explained that soldiers who encounter confrontations between settlers and stone-throwing Palestinians cannot determine whether the settlers are acting in legitimate self-defense. They should therefore give the settlers the benefit of the doubt and refrain from using lethal

---

[19] Foundation for Middle East Peace, *Report on Israeli Settlement in the Occupied Territories*, vol. 4, no. 3, May 1994.

[20] B'Tselem, *Law Enforcement vis-à-vis Israeli Civilians in the Occupied Territories*.

[21] David Hoffman, "Israeli Army Had Orders Not to Fire on Settlers," *Washington Post*, March 11, 1994.

[22] *Haaretz*,(Tel Aviv) March 11, 1994.

force. However, other testimony provided to the Shamgar Commission indicated that soldiers understood their orders as applicable not only to disturbances involving stone-throwing Palestinians, but to all situations in which settlers opened fire.[23]

That soldiers carry separate procedure booklets on the handling of Palestinians and settlers instead of a single set of rules for how to respond to particular offenses or dangerous situations is evidence of discriminatory treatment. The regulations concerning armed persons is revealing. With the exception of collaborators, Palestinians cannot legally carry weapons. The current IDF rules of engagement permit soldiers to shoot armed Palestinians on sight.[24] As Gen. Mofaz told the Shamgar Commission, "An Arab who is carrying a weapon is a terrorist. A Jew with a weapon is defending himself and he is allowed to shoot."[25] This reasoning gives settlers wide latitude to shoot at Palestinians with little fear of IDF intervention.

In many cases, soldiers have stood by and watched even when it was clear that militant settlers were using weapons for purposes other than defense. According to B'Tselem, frequently soldiers who witness acts of violence by Israelis against Palestinians make no effort to prevent or halt the attack. Nor do they pass on details to the police for investigation. There are cases in which soldiers not only do nothing to stop violence by settlers, but themselves join in attacks. [26]

The Israel Police

The Israeli police are responsible for investigating crimes committed by Jewish settlers against Palestinians in the territories. As early as 1982, an Israeli government commission of inquiry into police handling of settler violence, the

---

[23] The Commission concluded that while "the evidence does not suggest that anyone intended to prevent security personnel from opening fire on [any] individual who was committing a serious crime," it acknowledged "confusion" in the way that orders had been conveyed to soldiers. *Commission of Inquiry*, pp. 21-22.

[24] Middle East Watch, *A License to Kill: Israeli Undercover Operations Against "Wanted" and Masked Palestinians* (New York: Human Rights Watch, 1994), pp. 45-47.

[25] *Haaretz*, March 11, 1994.

[26] B'Tselem, *Law Enforcement vis-à-vis Israeli Civilians in the Occupied Territories*.

"Karp Commission," found "substantial deficiencies" in police conduct.[27] An "unacceptable" number of cases were closed on the grounds that "the offender is unknown," while in many instances no effort was made to locate the offender or to consult Palestinian eyewitnesses. More recent investigations confirm that this situation remains little changed. In response to a parliamentary question, Minister of Police Moshe Shahal stated that of forty complaints of settler violence registered between 1989-1992, twenty-six files had been closed and an additional four could not be located.[28] In only five cases had suspects stood trial. The remaining five cases were still under investigation.[29]

The high percentage of files closed suggests that issues raised by the Karp Commission remain pertinent: no investigations are conducted in some cases, and in others files are closed even though suspects have been identified. While the police are obligated to investigate all instances of settler violence that come to their attention, in practice they rarely initiate investigations unless a complaint is filed, even when soldiers or police have witnessed illegal acts.[30] Since many Palestinians do not report incidents of settler violence, most illegal acts by settlers are not investigated.

The reluctance to file complaints has many causes. Many Palestinians are loathe to report incidents of settler violence, because they fear settler reprisals, distrust Israeli authorities, or do not wish to recognize their authority. But when Palestinians have sought to complain, they have sometimes been prevented by security forces from entering police stations to file complaints. Such incidents have been documented by the human rights group HaMoked (The Hotline), the Center for the Defense of the Individual. Many cases pursued by HaMoked concerning settler violence are characterized by protracted investigations; "unlocated" files;

---

[27] *The Karp Report: An Israeli Government Inquiry into Settler Violence against Palestinians on the West Bank* (Washington: Institute of Palestine Studies, 1984).

[28] "File not located" covers cases in which no file was opened or files could not be found.

[29] Direct parliamentary interpellation on March 20, 1992 from Member of Knesset Dedi Zucker to the Minister of Police on investigation of offenses committed by Israelis against Palestinians; Minister's reply on July 11, 1993. Cited in B'Tselem, *Law Enforcement vis-à-vis Israeli Civilians in the Occupied Territories.*

[30] *The Karp Report*; B'Tselem, *Law Enforcement vis-à-vis Israeli Civilians in the Occupied Territories.*

and the closing of files on the grounds that the offender is unknown. Such results reinforce Palestinians' distrust of the Israeli police and discourage them from approaching authorities for assistance.

The Judicial System

In its report on settler violence, B'Tselem analyzed two aspects of the judicial system: the courts and the State Attorney's Office, which is responsible for bringing suspects to trial, plea bargaining, and appealing light sentences. While a lack of sufficient information precluded reaching definitive conclusions, B'Tselem's analysis points to the leniency with which both the State Attorney's Office and the courts respond to illegal behavior by Israelis against Palestinians.

In cases involving Palestinians killed by settlers, B'Tselem found that the State Attorney's Office closed a high percentage of cases due to insufficient evidence in spite of the fact that B'Tselem, which was not permitted to see the police files, had itself uncovered evidence that might have been useful in bringing charges against suspects in some of these cases. The State Attorney's Office also reduced charges from manslaughter to causing death by negligence in a number of cases as part of a plea-bargain. In several of these cases, B'Tselem concluded that the evidence against the defendant was solid and that there was therefore no apparent reason to agree to a plea-bargain. Finally, in cases where the court handed down light sentences, the State Attorney did not appeal even though it had previously sought rigorous punishment.

According to B'Tselem, of the forty-eight Palestinian fatalities committed by settlers between 1988 and 1992, twelve cases were brought to trial (representing fourteen fatalities, as two cases involved the death of two Palestinians each). In five of these cases, plea-bargaining reduced the charges from manslaughter to causing death by negligence. Of the twelve cases, one person was convicted of murder; one of manslaughter; and six of causing death by negligence. One was declared incompetent to stand trial; two (in a single trial) were convicted of lesser offenses; and one was acquitted. With the exception of the murder conviction, which carries a mandatory life sentence, all of those convicted received light sentences: the defendant convicted of manslaughter (which carries a maximum sentence of twenty years imprisonment) received a three-year sentence. Of the six convictions for causing death by negligence (which carries a maximum of three years imprisonment), the courts sentenced one defendant to eighteen months imprisonment; another to five months; and the four remaining defendants to periods of public service.[31]

Several judges have praised or expressed understanding for the ideological motivations of Israelis before announcing their sentences. In a case in which four Israelis were convicted of maliciously damaging property and trespassing, for having entered homes in the village of Imrin, beating residents, smashing windows and destroying furniture, Judge Amit wrote in his judgment:

> These are young settlers who, in this case, moved there, as I formed the impression, not to obtain a fine house cheaply, but because of their belief that the whole land of Israel belongs to the people of Israel. The defendants' belief and I suppose also their awareness of ... many acts of violence [committed by Palestinians] led the defendants, one can understand, to commit the offenses in this case.[32]

Palestinian defendants are virtually never released on bail; consequently they may spend months and sometimes more than one year in detention awaiting trial on suspicion of stone-throwing or other offenses. By contrast, settlers charged with violent offenses are routinely released on bail.

*   *   *

On February 25, 1994, Israeli settler Baruch Goldstein attacked Palestinians during their dawn prayers in the Ibrahimi Mosque in Hebron. Twenty-

---

[31] A life sentence was handed down by the Jerusalem District Court on April 28, 1994, against settler Yoram Skolnik. The defendant was convicted of premeditated murder for shooting a Palestinian as he was lying face down with his limbs tied behind his back. Joel Greenberg, "Jewish Settler Gets Life for Slaying Palestinian," *New York Times*, April 29, 1994.

[32] *State of Israel v. Anat Noked et al.*,C.F. 4/92, session 7, cited in B'Tselem, *Law Enforcement vis-à-vis Israeli Civilians in the Occupied Territories*. The B'Tselem report cites other examples, including *State of Israel v. Moscowitz,* C.F. 1440/92; *State of Israel v. Levinger,* C.F. 1872/88; *State of Israel v. Ishigayov,* C.A. 175/88; and *State of Israel v. Wallerstein,* C.F. 265/88.

nine Palestinians were killed and scores more injured[33] when Goldstein, dressed in army uniform, opened fire with a government-issued automatic rifle on the worshippers.

This attack, the bloodiest single event in the West Bank and Gaza Strip since Israel occupied them in 1967, called attention to the systematic failure of Israeli authorities to respond to violence by Jewish settlers in the same forceful manner that they respond to attacks on Israelis by Palestinians. It also highlighted the lack of protection afforded Palestinians. Testimony before the Shamgar Commission confirmed that security forces were concerned primarily with Palestinian attacks against Israelis and had not taken adequate measures to protect Palestinians from settlers.

Following the massacre, the Israeli government applied military orders, rather than domestic law, to incarcerate settler militants. Five were ordered administratively detained; eighteen were ordered not to enter Arab towns and to turn in their weapons. The government also banned two extremist organizations, Kach and Kahane Chai, which allows for the prosecution of persons who persist in being members, supporters, or financial backers of the groups. The implementation of these measures, however, does not demonstrate a commitment to curbing anti-Palestinian violence. Extrajudicial measures against a handful of extremists cannot substitute for a committed policy of preventing, investigating and prosecuting all acts of violence. It is also noteworthy that four of the settlers flouted the administrative detention orders and eluded the police for weeks; Kach leader Baruch Marzel was at large for one month after the order, during which time he appeared on radio talk shows.

According to data provided by the Minister of Police,[34] reported acts of settler violence doubled in 1993, surpassing all previous years. The police opened 312 files of violent incidents against Palestinians perpetrated by Israeli civilians. Given Palestinians reluctance to file official complaints, this probably represents only a small fraction of actual incidents.

As stated at the outset of this chapter, the government of Israel is in violation of international law by having facilitated the implantation and expansion

---

[33] More than 250 Palestinians were injured in the massacre and during the clashes and incidents that ensued that day, according to the Palestine Human Rights Information Center. PHRIC, *The Massacre in al-Haram al-Ibrahimi al-Sharif: Context and Aftermath*, a PHRIC Special Report (Jerusalem: PHRIC, May 1994), p. 2.

[34] Protocol No. 118, Knesset Constitution, Law and Justice Committee, November 22, 1993, p. 7.

of settlements in the West Bank and Gaza Strip. It is also guilty of condoning settler attacks on the persons and property of Palestinians by employing a double standard of justice. In contrast to its response to Palestinian violence against Jews, Israel fails to vigorously protect Palestinians from settler violence, and when illegal acts occur, they rarely receive vigorous investigations and even more rarely result in punishments commensurate with the crime.

SOUTH AFRICA

On February 2, 1990, State President F.W. de Klerk of South Africa announced the un-banning of the African National Congress (ANC) and other extraparliamentary opposition parties, the unconditional release of ANC leader Nelson Mandela, and the willingness of the National Party government to begin negotiations for the transfer of power to a government in which South Africa's black majority would have a part. The way seemed open for South Africa to overcome its repressive past and achieve a peaceful transition to democracy. Yet, despite the successful outcome of negotiations in all-race elections which finally took place from April 26 to 28, 1994, the four years of transition were marked by increasing violence rather than a new peace: at least 14,000 people died in political violence between February 1990 and April 1994. Although levels of violence have decreased dramatically since the election, many communities remain divided, uncounted thousands have been displaced from their homes, and in the newly established region of Natal-KwaZulu local government elections threaten to lead to violence perhaps equal in intensity to that which preceded the national elections of April 1994.

The great majority of outbreaks of violence pitted members of the ANC against followers of the Zulu-dominated Inkatha Freedom Party (IFP), led by Chief Mangosuthu Gatsha Buthelezi. In the worst affected areas—Natal Province and South Africa's industrial heartland around Johannesburg and Pretoria, known as the PWV region—many townships became divided into ANC and IFP camps, where trespassers from either side might be summarily executed simply for crossing invisible demarcation lines[1]. Squatter camps that mushroomed around the major urban centers as apartheid controls loosened became dominated by "warlords" who demanded absolute loyalty to the party of their choice. In rural KwaZulu, tribal authorities under the KwaZulu homeland government enforced a *de facto* ban on ANC activities. In many areas, households perceived to be linked to the ANC were driven out, in others, Inkatha-supporting chiefs were targeted for attack by ANC-aligned youth. In place of the familiar confrontations between the apartheid state

---

[1]Johannesburg and the area to its east and west is know as the Reef or, in Afrikaans, Rand, after the ridge in which the gold is found that is the foundation of the South African economy (the White Water ridge, or Witwatersrand). The greater urban area, including Pretoria to the north and Vereeniging and Vanderbijlpark to the south (which, with their townships, form the Vaal region), was known in shorthand as the PWV (Pretoria-Witwatersrand-Vereeniging) region. Following the election, the PWV region became one of the nine new regions and renamed itself Gauteng, after the SeSotho name for Johannesburg.

and its opponents, a more deadly conflict —often armed with sophisticated assault rifles imported from Angola or Mozambique—was played out between the members of South Africa's most deprived communities.

Although this conflict took place between political parties with differing ideological agendas, the violence was frequently portrayed by the media and indeed perceived by many of its participants as an ethnic or cultural struggle. In this interpretation, the ANC's utopian attempt to deny tribal identity and impose a socialist uniformity on South Africa's peoples had provoked Inkatha's defense of "traditional" Zulu values and respect for authority. Chief Buthelezi was the spokesperson for a Zulu culture that the ANC had ignored at its own risk.

Interpretations which analyze this violent conflict as primarily ethnically motivated, ignore the role of the South African government in fomenting strife between black South Africans. Tensions created or exacerbated by fifty years of rule by a government that chose race as the basis of policy were the necessary preconditions for the violence that frequently threatened to destabilize the transition process. Moreover, contemporary actions by state agents or by others acting with covert state support were central to its development.

Background

In retrospect, the hopes for a peaceful transition in South Africa raised by de Klerk's February 1990 speech were misplaced. Violence of the type that threatened the four years of negotiations was both predictable and, in fact, predicted. As far back as the 1960s, antiapartheid activists had warned that apartheid policies would result in a breakdown of law and order. The denial of political rights to black South Africans, the enforcement of a harsh system of migrant labor, the extreme restrictions on freedom of movement, the impoverished system of *bantu* education, the widespread detention of children, the forced relocation of stable communities, and the artificial emphasis on "tribal" identity, especially by the creation of "homelands" or *bantustans,*[2] were all factors that

---

[2] Under apartheid as originally conceived, all black South Africans would lose their South African citizenship and become instead citizens of theoretically independent states within South Africa's borders. Although all substantial ethnic groups of purely African origin in South Africa were eventually allocated to a particular homeland, the system was never entirely realized. Many Africans continued to live—legally or illegally—in areas officially designated for whites. Only four of the homelands (Transkei, Bophuthatswana, Venda and Ciskei) ever became nominally independent, and the other six (KwaZulu, KwaNdebele, QwaQwa, Lebowa, Gazankulu and KaNgwane) remained merely "self-governing territories." But though some avoided forcible

contributed to violence in South Africa.

The combination of economic immiseration, social disintegration and political repression resulting from these policies led to a brutal competition for resources between the poor and the very poor, the employed and the unemployed, those who lived in formal township housing and migrant workers from the hostels or shack dwellers from the squatter camps.[3] As the overt machinery of apartheid was dismantled and the most repressive laws repealed, the tight state control that had regulated all aspects of life was removed and the lid was taken off the boiling pot of black resentment created by these conditions.[4] No alternative democratic structures which might have mediated conflict had been established. Frustrations within black communities only grew worse as the drawn-out negotiations process failed to deliver visible results.

It was against this volatile economic and social background that the conflict between the ANC and the IFP developed. The ANC, South Africa's oldest political party, was formed in 1912 to challenge white minority rule and black poverty, initially seeking to achieve its aim through nonviolent negotiations." Following the victory of the National Party in white general elections in 1948 and the implementation of the systematically discriminatory policies of apartheid or "separate development", the ANC became more radical in its political program. In 1955, it adopted a "Freedom Charter" which included elements of an explicitly socialist program, and over the following years developed increasingly close links with the South African Communist Party (SACP). Banned in 1960, as a part of a crackdown on all forms of resistance to the government's policies, the ANC

---

removal, the homelands nevertheless became rural dumping grounds where unwanted black South Africans were sent to be ruled by nominally autonomous but repressive puppet black regimes.

[3] South Africa has one of the world's highest rates of criminal activity, with over 20,000 murders a year. A 1993 study published by the University of South Africa stated that the murder rate was 53.5 per 100,000. According to police statistics published in 1995, the murder rate is even higher, at ninety-four for every 100,000. Only a minority of such violence (from 10 to 15 percent of the deaths) is politically motivated. "South Africa has the highest murder rate," Reuters, August 27, 1993; "Shock murder figures for SA," *City Press* (Johannesburg), March 5, 1995.

[4] See, for example, Mike Morris & Doug Hindson, "South Africa: Political Violence, Reform and Reconstruction", *Review of African Political Economy* No. 53:43-59 (London, 1992) and Graeme Simpson and Janine Rauch, *Review of Political Violence 1991*, (Johannesburg: Centre for the Study of Violence and Reconciliation, 1992).

responded by proclaiming an "armed struggle" against the apartheid regime. From exile, its leadership called for the end of apartheid and the creation of a nonracial South Africa, waging a not very effective sabotage and bombing campaign within the country and supporting international sanctions and other measures in pursuit of that goal. With the Pan-Africanist Congress (PAC), it was recognized by the United Nations and the Organization of African Unity as the legitimate representative of the South African people.

Inkatha was a much more recent creation, founded in 1975 as Inkatha ya KwaZulu, a Zulu "cultural organization," though it claimed older roots as the revival of a 1920s organization of the same name. From the outset, Inkatha was more of a political party than a simple cultural movement. But although it adopted the symbolism and some of the rhetoric of the liberation movements and initially enjoyed a relatively close relationship with the ANC,[5] Inkatha's ideology was founded on a Zulu ethnic identity foreign to the ANC's determined nonracialism. Moreover, Inkatha opposed the ANC's armed struggle, its socialism and commitment to redistribution of wealth, promoting instead an ideology of free market capitalism and opposition to sanctions, and claiming a commitment to nonviolence on the basis of Christian principles. As a consequence of its conservative political stand, Inkatha enjoyed a privileged position as the only mass organization permitted by the South African government to speak on behalf of black South Africans, to hold rallies and to organize freely. Chief Buthelezi was hailed as the "moderate" black leader opposed to sanctions and boycotts, with whom the white minority could deal; the banned ANC was tarred with the brush of terrorist communism.

Overt conflict between the ANC and Inkatha developed in the mid-1980s, coinciding with an upsurge of protest against the white minority government. In 1983, the South African government implemented a new "reformist" constitution that gave members of the Indian and "Colored" (mixed-race) minorities the right to vote for segregated representative bodies parallel to the white parliament, but continued to exclude black South Africans from national government. The new structures were overwhelmingly rejected, and, in reaction to the continuing commitment of the government of P.W. Botha to the apartheid policies of his predecessors, despite its reforming language, over 500 antiapartheid organizations

---

[5]There is a longstanding dispute in accounts of the origin of conflict between Inkatha and the ANC about whether Chief Buthelezi took up the position of chief minister of the KwaZulu homeland and established Inkatha with or without ANC blessing. Nevertheless, for some years Inkatha was regarded by many as a surrogate for the ANC in Natal.

came together to form a nonracial coalition known as the United Democratic Front (UDF). For the next three years, the UDF was at the center of ever more militant resistance to the apartheid regime, coordinating "mass action" in support of the demand for black participation in government. Its avowed strategy was to make the townships ungovernable by the white regime. In 1985, the government responded to the threat of revolution by declaring a state of emergency, which lasted—with a brief interlude in 1986—until 1990. Tens of thousands of black South Africans were detained under the emergency laws, most of them during the peak years of repression from 1986 to 1988.

The years of emergency saw intensified conflict in many black communities, as differences emerged over the strategies of resistance. School or store boycotts, rent strikes and mass demonstrations, though largely popular, were sometimes imposed on an unwilling general population by radical enforcers of the UDF's protests. The lack of legitimate and democratic local government structures, coupled with the crackdown on the independent organizations of black civil society under the emergency, allowed individuals unaccountable to any constituency to assume power and impose their political preferences. Left to lead the struggle by the detention of more experienced leaders and the destruction of nongovernment channels of conflict resolution, increasingly militant youth targeted individuals regarded as collaborators with the regime. Black policemen came under attack, and many were forced to move out of the townships. Hundreds of black township councilors resigned, many of them threatened into their decision by the "necklacings" of some of their colleagues.[6] Others joined Inkatha, which backed black participation in the local government structures set up by the white government.

Inkatha opposed the mass action strategies of the UDF, in particular school boycotts and worker strikes, staking its position as a "moderate" and pro-business representative of black opinion. Although it had during the 1980s almost no claim to mass support on a national level, in Natal province and the KwaZulu homeland, the home of the majority of South Africa's Zulu speakers, Inkatha had a large membership. Clashes between Inkatha and students trying to arrange school boycotts took place in Natal from the early 1980s, and isolated confrontations between the UDF and Inkatha began to emerge almost immediately after the UDF's creation. In August 1985, conflict broke out in earnest when the townships of Durban saw the first serious clashes between UDF-supporting students and the

---

[6] "Necklacings" was the method of summary execution used in many cases of attacks on perceived "collaborators" with the regime: a gasoline-filled tire is placed around the victim's neck and set alight.

KwaZulu police or groups of Inkatha *amabutho*, or warriors.[7] By early 1990, many areas of Natal had become gripped by what was in effect a low-level civil war.

In this conflict, much of the violence took the form of a UDF/ANC rebellion against the Inkatha-controlled structures of the KwaZulu homeland, especially the system of tribal authorities controlled from the KwaZulu capital, Ulundi. Inkatha was threatened by the rise of UDF and the un-banning of the ANC not only because of its previously privileged status as the only mass black party recognized by the South African government, but also because of the commitment of the liberation movement to ending the homeland system and creating a unitary South Africa with a strong centralized government.[8]

Although formally a constitutional monarchy with an elected parliament, KwaZulu—the homeland created from enclaves within Natal for Zulu-speaking South Africans—became effectively a one-party state soon after its formal creation in 1972. Chief Buthelezi, president and founder of Inkatha, was also both chief minister and minster of police of KwaZulu. Many other high-level officials of Inkatha also held cabinet positions in the homeland. Inkatha membership was frequently required of residents of KwaZulu in order to obtain pensions, land to live on or schooling for their children. All public facilities were controlled by the government, and any organization allied to the ANC was forbidden from using meeting halls or other facilities. The structures of tribal government, following the pattern of indirect rule established by the British, were controlled from the KwaZulu capital of Ulundi and chiefs were expected to show absolute loyalty to Inkatha or risk replacement by more compliant representatives.

The conflict in Natal became in some respects one between the urban, better educated and more politically aware members of the ANC, demanding the

---

[7] As in other homelands, the planned redrawing of homeland boundaries to incorporate new communities was particularly contentious. Conflict first developed between Inkatha and representatives of several Durban townships attempting to organize resistance to rent and fare increases, when their Joint Rent Action Committee (JORAC) also coordinated resistance to moves to incorporate the same communities into KwaZulu. Attempts to incorporate the communities of Braklaagte and Leeuwfontein into Bophuthatswana, Nkqonkqweni into Ciskei and Moutse into Kwandebele also led to significant violence at around the same time.

[8] Many human rights monitors remarked that the violence practically served the IFP much more than the ANC. Inkatha (and the white right-wing) had the most to lose from the process of democratization and most to gain from the delays. See, for example, David Everatt, *Consolidated CASE Reports on the Reef Violence,* (Johannesburg: Community Agency for Social Enquiry (CASE), 1992).

right to speak on their own account, and the rural, often illiterate supporters of the "traditional" structures of government. Alternatively, as portrayed by the Inkatha itself and by the South African government, it was a violent revolt by the "lost generation" of township youth, radicalized by the communist ideology of the ANC to demand "liberation before education" and reject all discipline from tribal elders, against the proud representatives of traditional Zulu values and their respect for the established order. In ever more strident language, Chief Buthelezi repeatedly accused the ANC of wishing to destroy Zulu culture and pride, and portrayed the ANC's call for the dissolution of KwaZulu and other homelands as equivalent to the nineteenth-century defeat of the Zulu kingdom by the British.[9] While professing to support a strategy of nonviolence in opposition to white minority government, (by contrast with the ANC's open policy of armed struggle), Inkatha actively promoted an aggressive image of the "warlike" Zulu. "Cultural weapons" such as *assegais* or *knobkerries* were suddenly elevated to iconic status, and the proposal to ban their public display was vigorously opposed.[10] Any Zulu who was opposed to Inkatha's political program and world view was automatically branded

---

[9] In the course of multiparty negotiations, Chief Buthelezi and Inkatha agreed in principle to the reincorporation of all homelands into South Africa, but insisted on a large measure of local autonomy within Natal, to preserve the influence of Inkatha at the regional level. Accordingly, Inkatha argued that the new regions should become components of a federal system, with the power almost entirely devolved from the central government. In December 1992, the KwaZulu parliament published a draft constitution for a proposed federal region of KwaZulu/Natal. See Human Rights Watch/Africa, *"Traditional" Dictatorship: One Party State in KwaZulu Homeland Threatens Transition to Democracy* (New York: Human Rights Watch, September 1993), pp. 6-8.

[10] The carrying of "cultural weapons" had been banned by the British during colonial times, and remained banned until 1990, when the KwaZulu Legislative Assembly repealed three sections of the Natal Code of Zulu Law, originally drawn up by the British in 1891. The South African government repealed similar laws in effect outside the homeland. Following the signing of a Record of Understanding between the South African government and the ANC in September 1992, the government agreed to prohibit the carrying of dangerous weapons and to provide a mechanism for parties to apply to court for licenses to hold genuine cultural meetings. This agreement, described by the Buthelezi as a "cultural castration" designed to "destroy the Zulu ethnic identity and awareness", was never honored by the South African government. *"Traditional" Dictatorship,* Human Rights Watch pp 39-40.

as less than a Zulu.[11] The history of the Zulu kingdom was mobilized, with a cavalier disregard for accuracy, to bolster the claims to authority of the KwaZulu homeland and Buthelezi himself. A conflict that was political in essence became clothed in the powerful garb of cultural conflict.[12]

Despite the destructive conflict in Natal, other parts of South Africa remained largely unaffected by internecine violence of this type:[13] effective resistance to the state of emergency was crushed by 1989, and black residential areas returned to a relative if unstable calm. In February 1990, when President F.W. de Klerk lifted the state of emergency in all areas of the country but Natal, and announced the release of Mandela and the willingness of the government to

---

[11] There are approximately seven million people in South Africa who speak Zulu as their first language, making Zulus the largest single ethnic group. Although there was a powerful Zulu kingdom at the time of the British colonization of Natal, Zulus had never been united in one political unit before the creation of the KwaZulu homeland. Nevertheless, largely because the Zulu kingdom had a well-developed military system and was the only African polity to inflict a major defeat on the British army in the course of the colonization of the continent (at the battle of Isandhlwana in 1879), the Zulus became mythologized in British culture as the most "martial" of South Africa's African peoples. Chief Buthelezi was able to draw, if not explicitly, on this colonial literature in creating his vision of a unified and racially exclusive Zulu nation. Although tribal structures were used by other homeland regimes, particularly Ciskei and Bophuthatswana, to coerce support for the party in power, only in KwaZulu did the homeland political party gain real as well as coerced political support, a tribute to the power of the symbolism invoked by Buthelezi. Nevertheless, many Zulus obstinately refused to be united in this way. Quite apart from the urbanized Zulu-speakers living in the townships of the PWV or Durban, important cultural differences exist between Zulus..

[12] See, for example, Gerhard Mare, *Ethnicity and Politics in South Africa* (London and New Jersey: Zed Books, 1993). These cultural explanations had great force, resonating also with the received wisdom of white South Africans concerning the nature of African society generally and Zulu culture in particular.

[13] There were significant exceptions to this rule, such as the conflicts that broke out between leaders of different residents' associations in the Crossroads squatter camp near Cape Town in 1984, 1986 and 1988, in which scores of people were killed and thousands were driven from their homes. Cultural explanations of violence featured largely in the Goldstone Commission's report on the Crossroads violence, which described the dependence of new arrivals in the shantytown on "traditional" headmen. See footnote 18 for explanation of the Goldstone Commission.

enter into negotiations with the ANC, South Africans hoped for an end to civil strife.[14]

However, in August 1990, shortly after the ANC suspended its armed struggle and the negotiations process had formally opened, violence spread dramatically from Natal to the PWV area. For the next two years, many of the townships surrounding Johannesburg were torn apart by conflict, mostly between the ANC and Inkatha, which in December 1990 transformed itself from an explicitly Zulu cultural organization into a nominally nonracial political party, the IFP.[15] Most commonly, conflict developed between Inkatha-supporting Zulu migrant workers, housed in the barracks-like single-sex hostels built for them by the mines or industrial complexes, and the UDF/ANC "youth" who had led the township resistance to the emergency. Most victims, however, were simply ordinary residents of the townships, whose political or racial affiliation was unknown or unrecorded by those reporting on their deaths. Attacks on train commuters sowed terror on an apparently random basis, while "taxi wars" developed between rival associations of shared minibus taxis.[16] A revenge cycle of attack and counterattack developed in which massacres of large groups of people

---

[14] In October 1990, despite continuing problems in the region, Natal was also formally returned to normal "peacetime" laws.

[15] 8,312 people were recorded killed in political violence on the Reef from July 1990 to February 1994, an average of six a day, according to statistics compiled by the Johannesburg-based Community Agency for Society Enquiry (CASE) from reports in the media, by independent monitoring agencies and the police: David Everatt, Ross Jennings & Mark Orkin, *The Reef Violence: the Election Endgame* (Johannesburg: CASE, April 1994).

[16] Until the late 1980s, the government maintained strict control over any form of independent black economic activity, and all transportation was state-controlled. However, once independent minibus taxis were allowed, the government went to the opposite extreme and abrogated virtually any responsibility for regulation. Consequently, the market became glutted, leading to (literally) cutthroat competition, which often became politicized. In the townships of Cape Town, otherwise less troubled by political violence, "taxi wars" became the principal manifestation of conflict, but in many towns throughout South Africa commuters came to take their lives in their hands each time they decided how to travel to and from work.

at funerals or gatherings would be followed by reprisals and revenge.[17] Neither a National Peace Accord agreed in September 1991 nor meetings between Mandela and Buthelezi seemed to have any effect in encouraging peace.[18]

In contrast to Natal, where almost all the black population has Zulu as its first language, and conflict was therefore between Zulus of differing political opinions or cultural outlooks, violence in the PWV melting pot often took on an explicitly ethnic character. Existing tensions were exacerbated between long-time township residents, migrant laborers housed in mine hostels, and recent immigrants from rural areas living in "informal settlements" of shack housing. As rivalry between the ANC and Inkatha moved from Natal to the national level, Zulu migrant workers on the Reef were easily recruited to Inkatha.[19] The outbreak of

---

[17] According to the Human Rights Commission (HRC), a nongovernmental organization based in Johannesburg monitoring political violence and human rights abuses, sixty-one massacres (incidents in which ten or more people were killed at one time) were committed between July 1990 and June 1993. *Checkmate for Apartheid? Special Report on Two Years of Destabilization July 1990 to June 1992* (Johannesburg: HRC, 1993). See also, David Everatt, *Funeral Vigil Massacres: Mourning The Mourners* (Johannesburg: CASE, March 1992). (The Human Rights Commission has changed its name to the Human Rights Committee of South Africa, but keeps the same acronym.)

[18] The National Peace Accord was signed by twenty-seven parties to the political process, including the ANC, IFP, National Party government, business representatives and the police. The accord envisaged local and regional dispute resolution committees and a national peace secretariat which would monitor compliance with codes of conduct for political parties and the police and promote reconciliation between parties. The government also agreed to finance a socio-economic reconstruction and development component of the peace accord, to address some of the conditions that allowed violence to flourish. A standing commission of inquiry, the Commission of Inquiry Regarding the Prevention of Public Violence and Intimidation, headed by Richard Goldstone, an appeal court judge, was established in October 1991 under the Prevention of Public Violence and Intimidation Act 1991 and authorized by the signatories to the Peace Accord to investigate the background and reasons for violence.

[19] Already marginalized in township life and fearing a transition to an integrated economy no longer based on migrant labor, Inkatha offered these migrants protection from the threatened obliteration of their identity. Hostel dwellers, though amongst the most miserable victims of apartheid, had nevertheless established a lifestyle which depended on the continuation of the inhuman system of migrant labor, which the ANC wished to see ended. Maintaining a base and family in one of the homelands,

violence in August 1990 was attributed to an aggressive recruitment drive by Inkatha, in which non-Zulus, and especially Xhosas, who refused to cooperate with Inkatha were driven from the hostels. In the townships, despite the ANC's official nonracial ideology, Zulus became targeted as automatically representatives of the IFP, and many who had been uninvolved in any sort of conflict were driven out of previously ethnically mixed areas, often fleeing to the hostels. Impoverished and often uneducated residents of the squatter camps that sprang up with the relaxation of apartheid's "influx control" had been similarly marginalized from UDF/ANF organization, and were easily manipulated by "warlords" from either Inkatha or the ANC, often dividing entire areas along ethnic/political lines.[20]

The violence increasingly appeared to be linked to the progress of the multiparty negotiations: breakthroughs were often followed by attacks, while in June 1992 the killing of forty-two residents of the Vaal township of Boipatong resulted in the breakdown of the talks.[21] However, from late 1992 violence began

---

where they travelled for one month each year, migrant workers saw themselves as only temporary residents of the township hostels. Largely excluded from the township mobilization of the mid-1980s, their whole way of life was threatened by proposals for reform such as the conversion of the hostels to family units, or the abolition of the tribal authorities, on which their families depended. Lauren Segal, *The Human Face of Violence: Hostel Dwellers Speak* (Johannesburg: Centre for the Study of Violence and Reconciliation, 1991); David Everatt & Derek Schrier, *Hostel Violence in Soweto 22 July 1990 - 31 July 1992* (Johannesburg: CASE, 1992).

[20] Amongst the most notorious "warlords" were Thomas Shabalala, KwaZulu MP from Lindelani, a squatter camp outside Durban; David Ntombela, a KwaZulu MP from the rural areas bordering the township of Pietermaritzburg; and Jeffrey Nongwe, leader of the Western Cape United Squatters Association in Crossroads townships, later expelled from the ANC. See, Anthony de V. Minnaar, *Mafia Warlords or Political Entrepreneurs: Warlordism in Natal* (Pretoria: Human Sciences Research Council, 1991).

[21] The apparent tracking of the negotiations process was a phenomenon first remarked upon by the Community Agency for Social Enquiry (CASE) and later a truism of reporting on the violence. David Everatt, *Who is murdering the peace?* (Johannesburg: CASE, October 1991); David Everatt and Safoora Sadek, *The Reef Violence: tribal War Or Total Strategy?* (Johannesburg: CASE & HRC, March 1992). The Boipatong massacre became an emblem of the failure of the police to prevent political violence, and the focus of domestic and international attention on police methods. In March 1994, seventeen residents of the hostel were convicted of murder and attempted murder for this massacre. Eleven others were acquitted.

to decline in the PWV region, although it flared again in April 1993, following the assassination of Chris Hani, leader of the SACP and one of South Africa's most popular politicians. The exceptions to the downward trend were the townships of the East Rand, which in the second half of 1993—after the resumption of negotiations in April and the July announcement that all-race elections would go ahead in April 1994—were racked by some of the worst violence seen in the PWV area.[22]

Political and criminal violence increasingly overlapped: criminal gangs who adopted one or another political banner extorted protection money in the name of liberation while engaging in murderous internecine feuds; self-defense units (SDUs) set up with the encouragement of the ANC became undisciplined and preyed on the communities they were supposed to protect. Meanwhile, radical black groups opposed to the negotiations, such as the Azanian People's Liberation Army (APLA), the armed wing of the PAC, carried out attacks on whites, especially farmers in remote areas. Right-wing whites used increasingly violent tactics to demonstrate their resistance to the ending of white minority rule.

In Natal, conflict between the ANC and IFP steadily increased in intensity as the negotiations period dragged on. As the April 1994 election date approached, the province threatened to collapse into all-out civil war. After walking out of negotiations in August 1993, with several parties of the white right wing and the governments of Bophuthatswana and Ciskei, Chief Buthelezi of Inkatha maintained a boycott of the election process up to one week before the vote. Buthelezi claimed that the interim constitution agreed upon by the other parties to the process and passed by the white parliament in December 1993, gave too much power to the central government and insufficient autonomy to the nine proposed new regions that would replace the four provinces and ten homelands. Instead, Inkatha proposed an extreme form of federalism in which the regions themselves would choose how much power to cede to the center, stating that such a system was the only way to preserve local autonomy from a central domination by a godless and communist ANC.

Steadily increasing death tolls culminated in April 1994 with 337 killings

---

[22] According to the Human Rights Commission, 1,369 people died over the next six months on the East Rand in conflict between Inkatha-supporting hostel residents and township "self defense units" (SDUs) set up with the encouragement of the ANC. During the same period the HRC recorded the deaths of 191 people in the rest of the PWV region, an area much larger than the East Rand: Human Rights Commission, *Human Rights Review South Africa*, 1993.

recorded in the Natal/KwaZulu region.[23] Across the province, townships and rural areas saw levels of violence unprecedented even in the most troubled areas. Several thousand young men were openly given paramilitary training in "self-defence" at Inkatha camps in rural KwaZulu staffed by right-wing whites and KwaZulu police, and these paramilitary recruits were deployed in some of the most troubled areas. Concessions made by the ANC and NP, including a late agreement to hold separate regional and national ballots, failed to bring Inkatha into the process. International mediators came and left without success. Yet one week before the vote, Buthelezi dramatically switched positions and agreed to Inkatha's participation.[24] Violence immediately dropped to the lowest level in years, marred only by massive bomb blasts in the Johannesburg area, attributed to right-wing whites, which killed at least twenty-one in the final days before polling.

The Role of the South African Police
Throughout the negotiations period, the South African government maintained that the escalating political violence was caused simply by the rivalry between the ANC and IFP.[25] However, the central government was also responsible for continuing conflict. At a minimum, the South African Police (SAP) failed spectacularly in their duty to prevent acts of violence within black communities. The characterization of the violence as political enabled the police to evade their fundamental responsibility for maintaining law and order and preventing essentially criminal acts of murder, rape or destruction of property. In

---

[23]*Monthly Repression Report*, April 1994 (Johannesburg: Human Rights Commission, 1994).

[24] The reason for Inkatha's capitulation was not clear, although the premature departure of the last international negotiating team who refused to consider changing the election date, was certainly important. Others speculated that the last minute agreement to participate had been planned all along to ensure maximum disruption and minimum supervision of the poll in rural KwaZulu. Shortly after the elections, it also emerged that in a last minute deal the land composing the KwaZulu homeland had been signed over to the personal control of the Zulu king, Goodwill Zwelethini, by President F.W.de Klerk, an act that would be politically difficult for an ANC government to reverse.

[25] The view was buttressed by several widely criticized reports of the Goldstone Commission, dating from mid-1992, which stated that the primary cause of violence was ANC/IFP rivalry and minimized the responsibility of the state. Later Goldstone Commission reports substantially undermined this conclusion by detailing evidence of security force complicity in and incitement of violence.

the majority of instances of violence, no attackers were arrested, in the minority of cases where arrests were made few convictions were secured.[26] In just one example, Minister of Law and Order Hernus Kriel stated in September 1993, in response to a question tabled in Parliament, that only three people had been convicted in connection with 580 incidents of attacks on train commuters between July 1991 and May 1993.[27] In a report on the conduct of the police in their investigation of the Boipatong Massacre, British criminologist Dr.Peter Waddington commented scathingly on the lack of proper investigative procedures used by the SAP, even in a case subject to intense outside scrutiny, whose solution held serious political implications.[28]In many cases, human rights workers and community leaders claimed that a simple commitment to solving crimes and a moderately efficient use of existing resources could reduce vigilante justice, the cause of much of the violence, dramatically.

The police blamed their failure to solve crimes and stop the violence on the lack both of resources and of community cooperation. Almost all reports by outside experts agreed that the police force was understaffed and underequipped to combat the levels of criminal and political violence faced by a country in economic as well as political crisis. [29] Moreover, police training in South Africa,

---

[26]For example, in the course of an investigation into violence in Natal, a subcommittee of the Goldstone Commission reported that in Port Shepstone,on the south coast of Natal, "the bulk of [cases of murder, attempted murder and public violence] in the past two years...are still under investigation with no one being arrested and charged even where a suspect has been identified...Even in cases where charges have been brought there are inordinate delays in bringing matters to trial and the bulk of the accused in such cases have been released on bail. *Interim Report of the Wallis Sub-Committee of the Goldstone Commission*, dated August 31, 1993 but published March 18, 1994.

[27] Report in the *Star* (Johannesburg), quoted in David Everatt *et al, The Reef Violence.*

[28] Dr. P.A.J. Waddington, Director, Criminal Justice Studies, University of Reading, England, *Report of the Inquiry into the Police Response to and Investigation of Events in Boipatong on 17 June 1992,* Submitted to the Commission of Inquiry regarding the Prevention of Public Violence and Intimidation, July 20, 1992.

[29] In March 1995, Witwatersrand Attorney General Klaus von Lieres und Wilkau stated that the Witwatersrand region had 1.2 police for every 1,000 people, and that that nationwide the ratio was 2.5 per 1,000, against an international standard of 3 to

despite some reforms, remained focused on protecting the regime rather than the community and therefore failed to prepare officers for the task of criminal investigation. As a result, most South Africans were deeply suspicious of the apartheid regime's enforcement mechanisms, while witnesses were often too frightened to come forward for fear of retribution.

Questions of resources and training, however, could not fully explain repeated failures to take elementary steps to reduce violence. Well-known warlords suspected of serious crimes seemed to enjoy immunity from arrest and effective prosecution. Beyond lack of willpower and sheer negligence, it became increasingly clear that the police were deliberately failing to protect ANC-supporting townships that they had long treated as the enemy, and that they were consistently biased against the ANC and its allies.

Reports of police bias in responding to the violence multiplied with each escalation of the conflict. Time and again, eyewitness reports described the inaction of the police in the face of warnings of Inkatha attacks, police logistical support for vigilantes wearing Inkatha symbols, and crackdowns on ANC-supporting self defense units just before Inkatha attacks broke out.[30] In parts of KwaZulu policed by the homeland's own force, the KwaZulu Police (KZP), police support for Inkatha was virtually undisguised and the KZP came to be seen as the unofficial armed wing of the IFP.[31] In other cases the Internal Stability Unit (ISU) of the SAP, as the riot police were renamed, were accused of inflaming rather than suppressing violence, leading to demands for their withdrawal and replacement by

---

5 people per 1,000. "Shock murder figures for SA," *City Press*, March 5, 1995. According to the Independent Board of Inquiry, the police station in Thokoza, for example, had only two vans and one armored vehicle to patrol the entire township at the height of the violence during 1993. No detective unit was based at the police station, and cases had to be referred to other townships. Telephone lines to the police station were often out of order.

[30] Numerous domestic reports of police bias were confirmed by international observers. See, for example, Africa Watch, *The Killings in South Africa: The Role of the Security Forces and The Response of the State*, (New York: Human Rights Watch, January 1991); Amnesty International, *South Africa: State of Fear* (London, June 1992); International Commission of Jurists, *Agenda for Peace* (Geneva: June 1992).

[31] Legal Resources Centre (Durban) and Human Rights Commission (Durban), *Obstacle to Peace: The role of the KwaZulu Police in the Natal Conflict* (Durban: LRC 7 HRC, June 1992); Africa Watch, *"Traditional" Dictatorship*.

the once vilified but less politicized South African Defence Force (SADF). [32] As these reports multiplied, the more thoughtful leadership within the SAP was prepared to admit its problems in adapting from the ideology of a "total onslaught" from a communist-allied ANC;[33] however, more sinister evidence simultaneously mounted confirming allegations of covert government support for Inkatha and of the promotion of violence by elements of a "third force" intent on undermining the progress towards elections by the destabilization of black communities.[34]

Inkatha and the Government of South Africa

In June 1991, it emerged that Inkatha was benefiting from South African taxpayers not only as the party in control of the KwaZulu government, but as the recipient for many years of secret payments from the security branch of SAP. [35]

---

[32] In February 1994, following an ANC campaign after months of serious conflict in the East Rand, the ISU was replaced in Katlehong and Thokoza with the army. Violence dropped overnight to a fraction of its former levels.

[33] For example, the Wallis Sub-Committee of the Goldstone Commission, investigating violence in Natal, received a memorandum from the SAP in Port Shepstone which included the statement that "the SAP is aware that the complaints levelled against it are...not without foundation and accepts that some of its members have (a) displayed an anti-ANC bias; (b) attempted to discourage support of the ANC; (c) attempted to encourage support of the IFP; (d) committed acts of violence against the ANC; (e) refused to entertain complaints by ANC members; (f) turned a blind eye to violations of the law by members of the IFP; (g) abused their powers. In the turmoil that is wreaking havoc within the community, this conduct cannot be allowed to continue and the perpetrators of these acts must be rooted out before credibility and effective policing can be restored." *Interim Report of the Wallis Sub-Committee*, para 19.

[34] The term "third force" was adopted in South Africa to denote the belief that much of the violence was being fomented by organized interest groups other than the ANC or IFP. Although some have argued that there existed a centrally directed plan to destabilize the country, hatched by such a :third force" within the security forces, the term is used in general to refer to an uncentralized and often uncoordinated collection of disparate individuals or groups, some of them in the security services, each with its own agenda in promoting violence.

[35] In addition, the Inkatha-aligned and anti-sanctions United Workers Union of South Africa (UWUSA) was described in one internal police document as "a project under the control of the SAP." Revelations of covert government support for Inkatha were originally published in the Johannesburg *Weekly Mail* between 1990 and 1992.

The government attempted to explain the "Inkatha-gate" revelations as a legitimate tactic to counter the ANC's pro-sanctions stance, but there followed a succession of further allegations of police complicity in supporting Inkatha and provoking violence. In August 1991 President de Klerk was forced to confirm, in response to press reports alleging that the army and security policy had been involved in training hit squads in the KZP, that 200 Inkatha members had been secretly sent to be trained by the military intelligence division of the SADF in the Caprivi Strip in northern Namibia in 1986, and integrated into the KZP on their return. A much-criticized investigation by the Goldstone Commission concluded in June 1993 that "[t]here is no evidence at all to suggest that the SADF provided the training for the purpose of 'hit squads' being established." [36] But further investigations by the same commission into the situation in several townships in Natal and elsewhere culminated in a report published on December 6, 1993, which accepted the "high probability" that at least one hit squad had been operating in Natal, in which the leading figure was a Caprivi trainee.

Court inquests and official investigations establishes an additional series of links between the government and the provocation of violence. A police informer had participated in a well-publicized attack by ANC-supporting SDU members on hostel residents in the East Rand. [37] A massacre of eleven Inkatha

---

[36] *Report by the committee appointed to inquire into the allegations concerning front companies of the SADF and the training by the SDAF of Inkatha supporters in the Caprivi in 1986,* (Pretoria: Goldstone Commission, June 1, 1993), para 36.6. The report did, however, state (in para 36.3) that "training of the nature given to the trainees without having any regard to their subsequent control and deployment points to a grave error of judgement on the part of the SADF."

[37] In an attack on September 8, 1991, eighteen hostel residents in Thokoza township on the East Rand were massacred at a rally by members of the Self Defence Unit (SDU) based in the Phola Park squatter camp next to Thokoza. Although the SDU was not formally linked to the ANC, its members were themselves ANC supporters (though not members), while the ANC had encouraged the formation of SDUs in general. It was acknowledged by police in the course of an investigation by the Goldstone Commission that a police informer who was a member of the SDU was a section leader who had participated in the attack on the rally, and that the informer had led a "coup" by the SDU against the Phola Park Committee, a residents' association. *Report on the Inquiry into Violence at Tokoza* (Pretoria: Goldstone Commission, November 17, 1992), para. 18.

supporters attending a funeral vigil in the Natal Midlands had been carried out by a counterinsurgency unit of the SAP.[38] A well-known gangster responsible for many murders in the Vaal area had been a member both of the IFP and of the extreme right-wing World Preservatist Movement, and had apparently enjoyed police protection.[39] And a massacre of ten teenagers in northern Natal had been carried out by IFP supporters from the PWV and the investigating officer had been prevented from arresting those responsible.[40] In December 1992, following a

---

[38] On December 3, 1988, eleven people attending a night vigil were killed in the Trust Feeds area near Pietermaritzburg in the Natal midlands. Five policemen were eventually convicted of murder in April 1992 in connection with the attack. The court found that the massacre had been carried out by a unit created specifically to act against the UDF, as the "final event in a planned operation to disrupt a community, oust the residents' association and give Inkatha control of the defendants, who were special constables, stated that the attack had been planned in order to provoke a reaction from Inkatha against the UDF. Deneys Coombe, " 'Of Murder and Deceit': the Trust Feed Killings," in Anthony Minnaar (ed), *Patterns of Violence: Case Studies of Conflict in Natal*, (Pretoria: Human Sciences Research Council (HSRC), 1992).

[39] Victor Khetisi Kheswa, the "Vaal Monster," was suspected of complicity in numerous massacres in the Vaal area, including the killing of nineteen people in Sebokeng on the eve of the funeral of assassinated SACP leader Chris Hani. He was arrested and died in police custody in July 1993, amid allegations that he had been killed to prevent incriminating evidence emerging of police complicity in violence. John carlin,"Whites And Blacks Unite To Foil Democracy," *The Independent*, July 16, 1993; Alec Russell, "far Right Group Claims Link With Black Assassin," *Daily Telegraph*, July 14, 1993.

[40] The children were killed in November 1993 at the home of Chief Elphas Molefe of Nqutu, deposed by Chief Buthelezi for his support of the ANC. The incident was investigated by the Goldstone Commission after the KZP officer who had been removed from the case talked to the press. See *"Traditional" Dictatorship;* Human Rights Watch/Africa, *Impunity for Human Rights Abuses in Two Homelands: Reports on KwaZulu and Bophuthatswana,* (New York: Human Rights Watch, March 1994); Phillip van Niekerk, "Inkatha massacre cover-up" *The Observer* (London), March 6, 1994; *Interim report on Criminal Violence by Elements within the South African Police, KwaZulu Police and Inkatha Freedom Party,* (Pretoria: Goldstone Commission, March 18, 1994), para.22.

dramatic raid by the Goldstone Commission on Military Intelligence property, President de Klerk was forced to concede that SADF personnel had carried out "illegal and/or unauthorized activities and malpractices" that had resulted in deaths.[41]

Finally, on March 18, 1994, the eve of the election, the Goldstone Commission published a report which confirmed long-standing allegations that senior SAP officials (including both the deputy police commissioner and the head of police intelligence) had been involved in supplying Inkatha with weapons and financial support up to the very recent past. On March 22, a task force appointed by the Transitional Executive Council (TEC), to carry out an investigation into the operation of hit squads in Natal /KwaZulu delivered its report. It concluded that "hit squad activity in Natal and particularly in the area of jurisdiction of KwaZulu is rife. The number of deaths caused by these hit squads is unquantifiable but would represent a significant proportion of those who have died in political violence in Natal/KwaZulu."[42] A few days later, a further confidential report that was later leaked to the press identified senior KZP officers "whose conduct warrants investigation and, in some cases, suspension pending such investigation."[43]

Once Inkatha decided to contest the election, levels of violence immediately dropped: the election days themselves were amongst the most peaceful in years. However, widespread intimidation and fraud were reported, and

---

[41] Twenty-three senior SADF officers were dismissed as a result of the Goldstone investigations, although several notorious figures, including the head of MI, Gen. Christoffel van der Westhuizen, were left in office. An internal investigation into MI covert activities was instituted, headed by Lt.-Gen. Pierre Steyn, an officer with a relatively untainted record. The Steyn report was never released to the public, and only presented to Nelson
Mandela in July 1994, after the election.

[42] *Preliminary Report of the Transitional Executive Council Investigation Task Group into the Matter of Hit Squads in the KwaZulu Police, following from the Fourth Interim Report of the Goldstone Commission dated 6 December 1993*, TEC: Pretoria, March 22, 1994, para. 17. See also *Immunity for Human Rights Abuses in Two Homelands: Reports on KwaZulu and Bophuthatswana* (New York: Human Rights Watch, March 1994).

[43] *Second Interim Report of the Transitional Executive Council Investigative Task Group into the Matter of Hit Squads in the KwaZulu Police* (TEC: Pretoria, March 29, 1994), p. 1.

the final result—giving 50.3 percent of the regional vote to Inkatha—reflected a political compromise at national level rather than an accurate picture of voters' allegiances. Moreover, violence continued to simmer, especially in the rural areas, at what was regarded as crisis level a few years earlier. In January 1995, the number of deaths in political violence in the region reached 116, and many feared that the local government elections scheduled for October 1995 would also see the conflict between the ANC and the IFP escalating once again to the virtual civil war of March 1994.[44]

Despite the fact that the KwaZulu homeland was amalgamated with the former white province of Natal to form the new region of KwaZulu-Natal, the structures of the homeland—including the KZP and the chieftainship system—remained unchanged pending legislation to put in place a new police force and a restructured local government. Many of those named in the various reports of investigations into covert promotion of violence remained in office. Celani Mtetwa, a former minister in the KwaZulu cabinet implicated in gun-running by the Goldstone Commission report of March 18, became the new regional minister in charge of the police (from which position he vigorously resisted further investigation into hit squads). Gideon Zulu, a member of the royal family frequently linked with violence and hit squad activity, was appointed regional minister for welfare and pensions (an extremely significant post in the impoverished homelands). The Inkatha official in charge of the camps at which Inkatha *amabutho*, or warriors, had been trained before the election became a senator in the new national assembly. Those KZP police officers named in the TEC task force report of March 29 retained their jobs: six of the most notorious defied suspension orders from the new national Minister of Safety and Security.

Further revelations of "third force" activity confirmed the three March reports. In July, 1994, Gen. Roy During, the commissioner of the KZP seconded from the South African Police, stated that he was also aware of hit squads operating in the KZP but had been prevented from acting against them. In October, right-winger Riaan van Rensburg alleged that he had been hired by Walter Felgate, close advisor to Buthelezi, to train IFP members in assassination techniques. Moreover, it appeared that attempts to promote violence were continuing , with a view to disruption of the local government elections of October 1995. In February 1995, the graduation of a group of 600 recruits from the KZP training college at Ulundi was blocked by the national government after it emerged that at least forty of them

---

[44]The HRC recorded a total of 2,967 deaths in political violence during 1994, of which 1,602 were in Natal and 756 in the PWV region. 1,635, or 60.5 percent, took place before the election.

had criminal records and that only thirty-three were in fact qualified to join the police. It was credibly alleged that the recruits were intended to enforce support for Inkatha in the rural areas. Nationally, many of the highest ranking officers of the police and army most associated with the "dirty tricks" of the previous regime retired, but at lower levels allegations continued to be made of police partiality, especially in the SAP's Internal Stability Unit responsible for maintaining order in some of the troubled areas.

Investigations into covert activity by the security forces continued, and the ANC-led government of national unity formed after the elections committed itself to the formation of a "truth commission" to establish the full extent of the state and security forces' involvement in illegal activities aimed at undermining the resistance movements and destabilizing black communities, not only throughout the apartheid era but also in an attempt to derail the negotiation process. Nevertheless, full accountability for those activities remained unlikely: President Mandela promised a policy of "national reconciliation," while amnesty legislation was recognized by many as a political necessity to ensure the support of the civil servants and security forces of the old regime for the new majority government. While some resigned, many of those accused of involvement in "illegal covert action" against the ANC remained in office. The Inkatha official in charge of the training camps in Natal became a senator in the new national assembly; the official appointed to take charge of law and order in the new region of KwaZulu-Natal was amongst those linked to gun-running allegations; and many senior officials in the national security forces remained in office, despite being heavily implicated in allegations of covert action against the ANC throughout the negotiations period.

Conclusion

The destruction wrought by fifty years of apartheid government in South Africa created volatile communities easily divided by conflicts over control of scarce resources and the political agenda by which the state would in future be governed. In the months following the euphoria of the election, it became apparent that, although the immediate political objectives that had formed the basis of the conflicts of the negotiation period had been settled, violence would not cease simply as a result of an ANC victory. In the East Rand, violence continued to affect communities divided by years of semi-war, and "no-go" areas for either Inkatha or the ANC remained. In Natal, though the extreme violence of the pre-election period did reduce, lower level conflict continued into the next year, and local government elections threatened to fan the flames of violence to their previous heights. These conflicts could not be resolved without the successful implementation of proposals for economic and social reconstruction and development; the creation of legitimate structures of government, especially at the local level; but perhaps above all by the removal from positions of power of those who had deliberately promoted violence for their won ends. Although the full extent of responsibility for "third force" activities has yet to be established,[45] it is abundantly clear that action and inaction by members of the South African and KwaZulu security forces was directly or indirectly responsible for a significant proportion of the thousands of deaths in political conflict over the decade since 1985.

---

[45]In late 1994, the ANC-led government of national unity introduced legislation to establish a National Commission on Truth and Reconciliation, with a mandate to investigate gross abuses of human rights and to grant indemnity to individuals who made full disclosure of the acts for which they sought immunity from prosecution. The ANC's original proposals were watered down by the National Party and absolutely opposed by Inkatha and the white right wing. In March 1995, the bill was still bogged down in acrimonious discussions in the national assembly.

ROMANIA

An angry mob of ethnic Romanians and ethnic Hungarians from the town of Hădăreni lynched two young Roma (Gypsy) men and set thirteen Roma houses on fire on the night of September 20, 1993. The charred remains of a third Roma were found in one of the burned houses. The violence erupted after a fight, in which one of the Roma victims allegedly stabbed to death an ethnic Romanian man. The lynching occurred in the presence of two police officers who made no effort to intervene. Moreover, most of the thirteen houses were apparently set on fire after additional police officers had been deployed to the village. Reports indicate that the police did little to protect the homes and property of the Romas in the village. In November 1993 and May 1994, the chief prosecutor for Mureş county reported that there was sufficient evidence to issue arrest warrants for at least twelve individuals who were involved in the violent attacks on the Roma community in Hădăreni. Nevertheless, almost a year later, no one has been arrested or charged with a crime against a Roma victim.

The case of Hădăreni is not an isolated example. Since the fall of the Ceauşescu regime in December 1989, the Roma minority in Romania has become the frequent target of mob violence.[1] Over the last four and one-half years, an estimated 300 Roma homes have been burned, resulting in the temporary or permanent displacement of many Roma victims. Furthermore, ten Roma were killed during mob violence, and many others injured. Despite the extent of the violence against the Roma minority, and in clear violation of national and

---

[1] Since the Romanian revolution in December 1989, Human Rights Watch/Helsinki has conducted extensive fact-finding investigations into violent attacks on the Roma minority in Romania and the Romanian authorities' response to that violence. In October 1991, HRW/Helsinki issued *Destroying Ethnic Identity: The Persecution of Gypsies in Romania* which described in great detail many of these violent attacks, as well as the discrimination and hardships faced by Romas.

Prejudice against the Roma minority is a pervasive form of xenophobia, not only in Romania, but throughout the region. Shortly after the collapse of the communist regimes in Eastern Europe, violent attacks against Roma communities began to occur in many European countries. Studies have also shown widespread prejudice against the Roma minority throughtout the region. An important part of HRW/Helsinki's work to date has been the investigation and documentation of human rights abuses against Romas. In addition to our work on Romania, we have prepared the following full-length reports: *Destroying Ethnic Identity: The Gypsies of Bulgaria* (June 1991), *Struggling for Ethnic Identity: Czechoslovakia's Endangered Gypsies* (August 1992), and *Struggling for Ethnic Identity: The Gypsies of Hungary* (July 1993).

international laws[2], the Romanian authorities fail to take the necessary steps to defend Romas from mob violence and to aggressively prosecute those who carry out such violence. No Romanian citizen has been convicted of murder, arson, or physical injury that was committed during mob violence against a Roma community. Similarly, no police officer or local official has been charged with a crime relating to his involvement in the violence against Romas. The state fails to provide protection for Roma communities under attack, and makes little effort to provide an effective remedy for those Romas who have suffered personal injury or property damage.

The absence of an effective state response to the violence against Romas has substantially contributed to the continuation and escalation in intensity of attacks over the last years. Romas are made to understand that they have little hope of obtaining a remedy through the criminal justice system, and they often give up pursuing their cases. What is more, the non-Roma population has an increasing sense of impunity as years pass and no one is punished for the most serious crimes against Romas.

Background

The Roma population in Romania, which is estimated to be between two million and 2.5 million, constitutes the largest minority in the country (Romania's population is twenty-three million).[3] Romas are believed to have arrived in the region some time prior to 1300 A.D., having migrated from northern India between the tenth and eleventh centuries. While Romas share an ostensibly common heritage, it is difficult to speak of a single Roma population. The Roma minority is, in fact, composed of numerous distinct groups divided by language spoken, and

---

[2] Article 26 of the International Covenant on Civil and Political Rights (1966), to which Romania is a signatory, states that "all persons are equal before the law and are entitled without any discrimination to the equal protection of the law." International law is incorporated into domestic law according to Article 11(2) of the Romanian Constitution.

[3] According to the most recent census from 1992, there are 409,723 Romas in Romania, making up 1.8 percent of the population. However, this figure is widely believed to be inaccurate by both Roma leaders and the Romanian government. For a discussion of the difficulties in estimating the exact size of the Roma population, see Helsinki Watch, *Destroying Ethnic Identity: The Persecution of Gypsies in Romania* (New York: Human Rights Watch, 1991), pp. 5, 33-34. See also Elena Zamfir and Cătălin Zamfir, *Țiganii între Ignorare și Îngrijorare* (Bucharest: Editura Alternative, 1993), pp. 205-206.

whether they are or have been recently nomadic or are sedentary. [4]

Historically, Romas have suffered discrimination and mistreatment in Romania. In contrast to their treatment in many countries where they were banished, from the fourteenth century onward, Romas in the Romanian principalities were enslaved. In the mid-nineteenth century, with the growth of abolitionist sentiments in the Romanian principalities, slavery was finally abolished. Although some Romas fled the Balkans after the abolition of slavery and headed toward Western Europe and on to North America, many remained in the areas where they had been slaves and ultimately sold themselves back to their former masters because they had no means of providing for themselves or their families.

Under the pro-Nazi government of Marshall Ion Antonescu, which came to power in 1939, many Romas, and particularly nomadic Romas, were deported to occupied territories in Transnistria and the Ukraine. According to the Romanian War Crimes Commission, set up by the Romanian People's Court after World War II, 36,000 Romas died during the war period. While the majority of these deaths were due to hunger, exposure to freezing weather, and typhus, a significant number were killed by the Romanian gendarmerie.[5]

The Socialist Republic's Assimilationist Policies Toward Romas

In theory, the Socialist Republic of Romania established guaranteed fundamental rights to all Romanian citizens without regard to ethnic origin. However, in practice, these rights were subordinated to the objectives of the Romanian Communist Party (RCP) and its leadership. In the name of modernization and "homogenization", or leveling, of society, the RCP leadership adopted a series of polices that had a negative impact on the Roma minority and over time contributed to an escalation in tensions with the majority population. Because Romas were viewed as a primitive and backward people who were an embarrassment to efforts to create the modern socialist state, the Romanian government set about to forcibly modernize and assimilate the Roma minority.

For the Roma population, these new efforts at social engineering were

---

[4] Most Romas in Romania are now sedentary. Those who were still nomadic at the end of World War II were forced by the government to settle. However, an estimated 10 percent of the Roma population still travels during the warm months of the year.

[5] Donald Kenrick and Grattan Puxon, *The Destiny of Europe's Gypsies* (Sussex University Press, 1972), p. 128. See also J. Schechtman, "The Gypsy Problem," *Midstream* (November 1966), p. 57.

especially onerous. New laws and regulations mandated certain behaviors that were inconsistent with the traditional Roma lifestyle. The effect of these changes in state policy was to destroy the traditional Roma lifestyle and traditional professions, and to bring the Roma minority into greater conflict with state institutions.

As early as the late 1940s, the Romanian government attempted to control where and how Romas lived. By the early 1950s, the government had begun to forcibly settle those Romas who were still nomadic, using a variety of measures such as the confiscation of horses and wagons. According to Romanian law during the Ceauşescu era, every citizen was required to have a permanent, registered address in order to receive certain benefits such as rationed goods or free medical services. However, efforts to settle nomadic Romas were never completely successful, and constantly led to conflict between some Romas and the police who were responsible for the policy's implementation.

In 1951 the Ministry of the Interior began to disperse compact groups of Romas so that they could be more easily monitored by the police.[6] Some Romas were forcibly settled on the fringe of existing villages. But established residents of these areas resented the influx of Romas, and Romas found integration into these communities difficult.

In the 1980s, Romas were targets of Ceauşescu's "systematization" program, which called for the razing of whole districts, especially those with run-down, older houses, and the construction of modern, high-rise apartment buildings in their place. Whole Roma areas were destroyed, and large groups of Romas were relocated in various large, modern buildings. Although the "systematization" program was intended to provide all Romanian citizens, including Romas, with improved standardized housing, the results were devastating as the traditional Roma neighborhoods were destroyed and Romas were concentrated in blocks of flats, in urban ghettos.

The Ceauşescu government also had a policy of moving Romas into houses confiscated from emigrants. This policy created enormous resentment among non-Roma neighbors and a great deal of social tension. For example, in the town of Sibiu, Romas were given the homes of Germans emigrating to the Federal Republic of Germany. As one ethnic Romanian woman recalled: "Ceauşescu put Gypsies in German communities. It was not long before the houses were ruined.

---

[6] "Comuna Mihail Kogălniceanu - " *EXPRES* (Bucharest), October 30, 1990.

This was viewed as a way to destroy the whole German community."[7]

The tensions produced by these forced settlement and relocation programs grew over the years and were even exacerbated by later economic developments. The government's assimilation policies caused increasing tensions between Romas and non-Romas, the full extent of which is only now being felt. Several of the Roma areas attacked during the last years were areas where Romas were settled after 1950. Similarly, ethnic hostilities grew over time and were exacerbated by the fact that they could not be acknowledged and addressed publicly. By the 1980s, the Ceauşescu government had announced that the minority question in Romania was resolved. It became less and less acceptable to even identify problems in terms of ethnic groups.   After the revolution of 1989, individuals again had the opportunity to express their resentments and anger, and such expressions were all the more intense for having been repressed for decades. In addition, in the period immediately following the revolution, some citizens felt a general disrespect for the legal order and were willing to take matters into their own hands. The Romanian state's unwillingness to take a strong position against vigilante violence targeting Romas led to a particularly explosive situation.

Violence Against the Roma Minority in Post-Ceauşescu Romania

The increase in prejudice against the Roma minority during the 1970s and 1980s exploded into full-fledged violence after the fall of the Ceauşescu regime in 1989. Ethnic tensions found expression in ethnic violence immediately following the revolution. Although these ethnic hostilities may be partially explained by historical developments, the continuation and escalation of the violence against Romas over the last four years is largely the result of a passive, and often tacitly hostile, state response to attacks against the Roma minority.

Violence against Romas has occurred in geographically dispersed areas, but the attacks follow a common pattern. In most instances the mob violence was sparked by a crime allegedly committed by a Roma, or an argument between an individual non-Roma and a Roma. These conflicts were frequently the result of a high consumption of alcohol, and often occurred outside a bar or night club. The villagers were frequently called together by the village alarm or church bells, which also served to warn the Roma community that an attack was imminent. The violence was intended to force Romas out of the village and, by destroying their houses, to prevent them from returning.

---

[7] Human Rights Watch/Helsinki interview, Sibiu, September 1991, quoted in *Destroying Ethnic Identity: The Persecution of Gypsies in Romania*, p. 23.

Police Failure to Protect Romas

In almost all cases of violence against Romas, the police have failed to provide any protection to the homes and property of Roma families, even when they were aware of the likelihood of violence.[8] For example, in the town of Ogrezeni, a violent attack on May 17, 1991 resulted in the destruction or burning of twenty-one Roma houses. Romanian eyewitnesses to the violence reported that the police were patrolling the area when the houses were set on fire, but did nothing to stop the villagers. Similarly, in Hădăreni (discussed above at p.63), between forty-five and sixty armed police officers arrived in the village after the first Roma house was set on fire, but more than two hours before the additional twelve houses were burned. Yet, these police did nothing to stop the arson.

In some cases the police or local officials were accused of participating in the violence by calling the villagers together and urging them to attack Romas and/or their property. For example, in the town of Cîlnic near Sibiu, Romas reported that the Romanian villagers who attacked their quarters were accompanied by police and that the police did not intervene when the villagers attacked Romas' houses. The local mayor did not deny that police had been present when the attack occurred. Similarly, there is substantial evidence that the mayor and the local priest in Bolintin Deal where twenty-two Roma homes were burned in April 1994, were, at the very least, aware of the villagers' plans to attack the Roma quarters and took no steps to call the police or prevent the violence, and there was some testimony alleging that the police directly instigated the violence.

The police response to these violent attacks often reveals intentional bias in favor of the non-Roma population and outright hostility toward the Roma minority.

Police malfeasance is frequently tolerated and even condoned by superior

---

[8] States have an obligation to protect all citizens from violence, including a specific obligation to protect minorities from violence due to racial or ethnic identity. Article 5 of the United Nations International Convention on the Elimination of All Forms of Racial Discrimination states:

> States Parties undertake to prohibit and to eliminate racial discrimination in all its forms and to guarantee the right of everyone without distinction as to race, color, or national origin, to equality before the law, notably in the enjoyment of . . .

> b.   The right to security of person and protection by the State against violence or bodily harm, whether inflicted by Government officials or by any individual, group, or institution . . .

officers and prosecutorial officials responsible for opposing and punishing such behavior. No police officer has been investigated for failure to take the necessary steps to protect Romas, and there have been no criminal investigations of police participation in mob violence. Few police officers have even been disciplined by their superior officers for failing to carry out their duties. Only in the Hădăreni case, which occurred one week before Romania's application for membership was to be considered by the Council of Europe, were police officers disciplined for the failure to respond properly to mob violence.

Even in cases where the violence is initiated by representatives of the state, individual perpetrators are rarely prosecuted. For example, on July 3, 1992, approximately thirty-five soldiers (Military Unit 02180) in uniform and with rubber clubs left their barracks and went to Piața Rahova, in an area of Bucharest. When they arrived they proceeded to beat up several Romas working in the area. Nine Romas filed complaints, and three of them suffered injuries requiring medical care. One Roma woman also suffered substantial property damage. The attack was apparently motivated by a fight that had taken place two days before between one of the military officers a Roma man. The evidence gathered from Roma witnesses interviewed by Human Rights Watch indicates that the soldiers went to the area on their own initiative and that they were not attacked by the Romas in the square. What is more, there was testimony from the chief military prosecutor that the soldiers viewed the "action as a gesture of camaraderie" with the officer who had been injured. Despite this evidence, however, the military prosecutor announced that no charges would be brought against any of the soldiers because they had acted in "legitimate self-defense."

Failure to Investigate and Prosecute Attacks Against Romas
Only a handful of individuals have ever been charged with crimes related to mob attacks on the Roma community. In many cases, the investigation has dragged on for years without the prosecutors or police being able to identify the perpetrators. The circumstances of mob violence, where the police and local officials are often present, make it incredible that the prosecutorial authorities are unable to identify a single person involved.

Instead, it appears that the police and prosecutors assigned to these cases are not particularly motivated to resolve them, or are actively opposed to doing so. It appears that both the local police and prosecutors use a variety of techniques to delay and sidetrack the prosecution of cases where the victims are Romas.

In some cases the police and prosecutors fail to identify and collect evidence and testimonies immediately after the crime takes place. Instead, months and even years go by and the evidence is ultimately lost or, by the time it is collected, substantially less probative in value. There is also evidence that some prosecutors interview only or primarily the perpetrators and never take the statements of the victims, especially in cases where the victims are able to identify some of the perpetrators. For example, almost three years after the violence in Bolintin Deal only two victims had been interviewed. The police had made little effort to identify the victims or to collect evidence for the case. In May 1994, due to pressure by domestic and international human rights organizations, as well as representatives from the Council of Europe, twenty-three victims were interviewed in a one- month period. By contrast, when a Roma is accused of having committed a criminal offense, the police and prosecutors operate with maximum speed and efficiency.

Although difficult to quantify, there also appears to be a distinct tendency by the police and prosecutors to discount the testimony of Roma eyewitnesses or victims solely because they are Romas. Many of the prosecutors involved in cases of mob attacks on Roma communities convey a distinct bias in favor of the uncorroborated statements of the majority population.

Another common strategy is to interview the victims repeatedly over the course of several years, calling them back to question whether they still want to pursue their cases. After years of dealing with the authorities without any progress, many Romas ultimately lose interest in pursuing their complaints and drop all charges.

In general, there is pressure on Romas to settle the cases. Roma frequently appear to be threatened that they will not be able to return to their homes if they pursue the criminal case. Alternatively, government officials pay for the reconstruction of Romas' houses in apparent exchange for the victims' agreement to withdraw their complaints. For example, Romas in the town of Turu Lung reported that police told them they would not be able to return to their homes if they did not withdraw their complaints. Ultimately, the houses were built with government funds and the complaints were withdrawn.

While it is common practice to settle a case by mutual agreement, that agreement should be between the parties to the conflict. It is improper for the state to negotiate a settlement directly with the victims, offering state funds in exchange for withdrawal of criminal complaints, and thereby indicating a lack of independence and objectivity. It is also improper for the state to make the right of Romas to return to their homes dependent upon their agreement not to pursue their criminal cases.

In those few cases in which charges have been brought, they have been for relatively minor offenses. This is especially important because minor offenses require a complaint by the victim in order for the prosecutor to begin an investigation. There is evidence that some prosecutors intentionally charge the perpetrators with lesser crimes than warranted by the evidence so that there will be no legal barrier to settling the case, even though the victims may have indicated repeatedly that they do not wish to settle.

Those cases that actually progress to the point of trial often languish in the courts for years without resolution. For example, in the case of Kogălniceanu, where thirty-three Roma houses were burned or destroyed in October 1990, trial did not begin until June 1992 and, as of January 1995, had not been completed. The trial has been delayed, in part, because the defendants and witnesses refused to appear in court to testify. Attorneys representing the Romas have repeatedly complained that the police do nothing to ensure that those called to testify will actually appear in court. Numerous requests that the police guarantee the appearance of witnesses had gone unanswered.

The Romanian state, by failing to punish promptly and thoroughly those who have participated in mob violence, denies the victims the equal protection of Romanian law. Considering the enormous cost in human suffering, the uprooting of lives and the costly property damage involved, this is an abhorrent failure by the Romanian justice system. Despite the efforts of Roma leaders and human rights activists, many Romas no longer see a benefit to filing complaints when they are victims of violence. They have become impatient and frustrated, and have no faith that their rights will be protected by state institutions.

Similarly, the Romanian state has provided no deterrent for those who would choose to participate in such violence in the future. On the contrary, many villagers feel encouraged to attack their Roma neighbors specifically because of the state's passivity in such cases. For example, after the violence in Hădăreni, villagers referred repeatedly to similar attacks in Kogălniceanu and Bolintin Vale, pointing out that no one in those cases had been held legally responsible for violence against the Romas living there.[9]

Anti-Roma Prejudice in the State-owned Broadcast Media

The government's own bias against the Roma minority is also conveyed in a less direct, but equally effective way, through the state-owned broadcast media. The state-owned television, which is the only national television channel in Romania, consistently portrays Romas as criminal elements who are the cause of all Romania's economic and social problems. "The Romanian media, reflecting a

---

[9] Asociaţia Pentru Apararea Drepturilor Omului În Romania - Comitetul Helsinki, "Report on the APADOR-CH Fact-finding Mission to Hădăreni and Târgu Mureş (October 5-7, 1993), p. 6.

general public attitude among Romanians, often depict Gypsies as thieves, beggars, and black marketeers, or as people who do nothing but cast spells, make curses, and foretell the future."[10]

State-controlled television has also been accused of inciting the Romanian population to violence by its often inaccurate and inflammatory portrayal of Romas. For example, on June 13, 1990, during anti-government demonstrations, the director of the television services, Emanoil Valeriu, announced on the air, falsely, that the television studios had been attacked and destroyed by Romas and called on the Romanian population to protect and defend the institution. During the following two days, June 14-15, vigilante mobs of miners arrived in Bucharest and, among other things, sought out and attacked Roma quarters around Bucharest.[11]

The state-owned television has also been particularly manipulative in its reporting on violent attacks on Roma communities, introducing many such reports with long descriptions of the horrible Romas who live in the affected villages. For example, "in its coverage of the events in Hădăreni, one television report stated that the pogrom came about 'after a long period of tension between the villagers and the Gypsy community caused by robberies and aggressive actions taken by the Gypsies.'"[12]

The Government's Failure to Guarantee Equal Protection for Romas

Although attacks on Romas began immediately after the December 1989 revolution, the new Romanian government was slow to condemn such abuses and did not firmly and clearly disassociate itself from those participating in the attacks. On the contrary, government officials have often appeared to sympathize with the perpetrators by repeatedly attempting to explain why the majority population resorted to the violence.

The Romanian government has been slow to take a public position against the violence and for the unconditional right of the Roma victims to return to their

---

[10] "Special Report: Gypsies in Eastern Europe," Soviet/East European Report (Radio Free Europe/Radio Liberty Vol. VII, No. 39, August 1, 1990), p. 1.

[11] For a complete description of these events, see Helsinki Watch, "News From Romania: Violent Events of June 13-15," *a Human Rights Watch Short Report*, July 1990.

[12] Adrian Bridge, "Romanians vent old hatred against Gypsies," *The Independent*, October 19, 1993.

homes. Senior Romanian government representatives have indicated that, at least in the short run, they could not force the non-Roma majority to accept the Romas back into their villages. Instead, this should be handled at the local level. The government's total abdication of responsibility for the safety and security of Romanian citizens of Roma ethnicity, especially in the months immediately following the revolution, sent a clear signal to those at the local level that they would face no repercussions if they chose to ignore their legal obligations.

The Romanian government has taken the position that the violence against Romas is "social" in nature and does not result from anti-Roma prejudice. This argument is a barely concealed effort to downplay the seriousness of the violence and to place the blame on the victims themselves for their suffering. The government has emphasized that violence against Romas is local, limited in scope, and imputed to unique and individual circumstances."[13] In addition, the Romanian government attempts to justify or downplay the violence as "spontaneous" outbursts by villagers that are the result an "accumulation in time of bad, deviant and illegal behavior of Romas."[14]

Over the last year, the Romanian government has responded somewhat to international pressures by speaking more forcefully against violent attacks on the Roma minority. For example, the government immediately condemned the violence in Hădăreni. However, even in the context of such condemnation, the government tried to place the blame on the Romas. In the case of Hădăreni, the government stated:

> The Government of Romania noted with concern the events in the village of Hadareni-Chetani, county of Mures, that resulted in human losses and destruction of property that afflicted, in particular, the Roma families illegally settled in the area. Their behavior, culminating in the cold-blooded killing of a young man, stirred the spontaneous reaction of the other inhabitants of the village, both Romanians and Hungarians, that degenerated

---

[13] Romanian government statement made at the CSCE meeting in Copenhagen, June 1990.

[14] Ibid.

into acts of violence.[15]

Equally telling, the government promised that in the Hădăreni case measures would be taken to "investigate the case and bring the incriminated persons to trial." However, eighteen months after the violence and over a year after the prosecutors indicated that they had sufficient evidence to issue arrest warrants, no one has been charged with a crime in that case. The local officials responsible for the prosecution of the case have stated that they are under political pressure, apparently from local political leaders, to delay issuing arrest warrants. The national government has apparently taken no steps to ensure that the local prosecutors are able to carry out their responsibilities without political interference.

The government's failure to condemn the violence firmly and clearly and to show that those who commit crimes against the Roma minority will be promptly and thoroughly investigated and tried contribute to the majority population's sense that they have impunity to commit acts of violence against Romas.

Conclusion
The violence against the Roma minority is, in part, the long-term effect of state policies that created and manipulated social and ethnic tensions without providing a legitimate means by which to express and resolve hostilities. Ethnic tensions had long been exacerbated by the heavy-handed social engineering of the Ceauşescu regime generally, and targeted at minorities specifically. Although some of these policies were intended to benefit and improve the lives of Romas, the effect was often disastrous. The assimilation and relocation policies destroyed much of the Roma minority's traditional lifestyle and means of living and forced them to settle in areas where they were unable to integrate and were unwelcome by those already living there.

Since 1989, the Romanian goverment's response to violence against the Roma minority has contributed to a growing sense of impunity among non-Romas, as well as a growing sense of insecurity among the Roma minority. In 1990 and 1991, as the number of attacks against Romas escalated, the government was slow to condemn the violence and to disassociate itself with those expressing anti-Roma sentiments. Although the government now condemns violent attacks against the Roma community, it simultaneously tries to downplay the seriousness of such

---

[15] "Statement of the Romanian Government Regarding the Events in the Village of Hădăreni-Cheţani, County of Mureś, September 20-21, 1993," September 23, 1993, p. 1.

attacks, by focusing on the high crime rate in the Roma community and the suffering of the non-Roma population that has to live together with Romas. The Romanian government's statements attempt to shift blame away from the perpetrators of the violence to the victims themselves. The state-owned broadcast media reinforces the anti-Roma sentiment. It not only portrays Romas in a negative light, but its reports on violent attacks against Romas are often inaccurate and highly inflammatory.

The Romanian government's failure to treat the violence against Roma as a serious problem is reflected in the response of other state institutions as well. The police and the prosecutorial bodies have consistently failed to protect Romas from violent attacks and have denied them a prompt and adequate remedy for the crimes committed against them. The failure to promptly and agressively investigate, charge and prosecute those who have committed crimes against the Roma minority sends a clear message: the Roma minority in Romania cannot expect and does not receive the equal protection of Romanian law.

SRI LANKA

For many observers, decades of violence among Tamils, Sinhalese, and Muslims epitomized Sri Lanka's seemingly endless cycle of ethnic strife. A series of ethnic riots from 1956-1983 claimed hundreds of lives. In 1983 began a civil war in which loyalties were defined largely by ethnicity in Sri Lanka. That war has killed some 30,000 people. Participants in this conflict engaged in massacres targeting particular ethnic communities along Sri Lanka's eastern coast and in the northern part of the island. But many of these killings were more than spontaneous outbursts of communal enmity; many were systematically carried out by the state and other important actors in the civil war for political ends.

Sri Lankan government forces and militant Tamil separatists, most notably the Liberation Tigers of Tamil Eelam or LTTE both fostered and committed acts of ethnic violence to gain popular support, secure territory and isolate their enemies. Successive governments promoted impunity for members of their forces who engaged in violence for political and military ends.

In the course of the war, members of Sinhalese and Muslim civilian militias called "home guards," armed by the government and ostensibly deployed to protect vulnerable communities, engaged in large-scale killings in Tamil villages. Anti-LTTE Tamil militants were similarly deployed by the government for counterinsurgency. These groups, acting alone or in concert with Sri Lankan security forces, engaged in massacres, disappearances, torture, and extrajudicial executions. Many of these abuses appear to have been perpetrated based solely on the victims' ethnicity, with the aim of rooting out LTTE fighters, discouraging local support for the LTTE, or driving Tamil villagers out of the area.

Tamil separatists have also engaged in targeted political violence and large-scale massacres of Muslim and Sinhalese civilians living in or near Tamil-dominated areas. In 1990 the LTTE sponsored the wholesale forced eviction of Muslims from areas of northern Sri Lanka under their control. These acts were apparently designed to prevent the groups from gaining political influence, or establishing alliances that could benefit government forces.

Background

Sri Lanka is home to an ethnically diverse population of about seventeen million. Its geographical position at the juncture of important trade routes which linked India, Southeast Asia and the Middle East, and its colonization over hundreds of years by the Portuguese, the Dutch and the British, contributed to the development of many unique communities.

Most Sri Lankans consider themselves to belong to one of four major ethnic groups, Sinhalese, Sri Lankan Tamil, Indian Tamil, and Muslim or Moor.[1] Most Tamils are Hindu and most Sinhalese, Buddhist, but there are also significant numbers of Tamil and Sinhalese Christians (mostly Catholics). The Sinhalese, who are the majority community and speak Sinhala, constitute approximately 74 per cent of the population. Sri Lankan Tamils, about 12 percent of the population, speak Tamil, which is also spoken by more than fifty million people in the southern Indian state of Tamil Nadu. Most Muslims, who comprise about 7 percent of Sri Lanka's population also speak Tamil as their mother tongue, but they are generally treated as a separate ethnic group based on their religion; Indian Tamils make up about 6 percent of the population.[2] There are also several smaller minority groups, such as the Burghers, who are of European descent; Malays (who are also Muslim); and Veddahs (or Väddas), thought to be descendants of the island's earliest inhabitants.

Since independence, the primary conflict has been between the Sinhalese and Tamils. During the initial stages of the conflict, the question of language rights was the key area of contention between these communities. Before independence in 1948, under two centuries of British colonial rule, English was the language of commerce and administration. The majority of Sri Lankans were thus excluded from the process of government, but because English served as a bridge language between ethnic groups, minorities, particularly Tamils, filled many civil service positions.

Sinhalese activists charged that English-educated minorities wielded disproportionate power on the national level, and that Buddhism and the culture associated with it lacked protection as long as its supporters were excluded from governing. Tamil activists, on the other hand, resented a perceived tendency on the part of Sinhalese partisans to equate their own ethnic nationalism with Sri Lankan

---

[1] Concepts of ethnicity are subject to change. In the past there was an important distinction drawn between Kandyan and coastal Sinhalese. Jaffna Tamils have certain cultural differences from other Tamils. In the recent past, Tamil political groups attempted to include both Indian Tamils and Muslims with Sri Lankan Tamils in a single category, "Tamil-speaking people." This proved largely unsuccessful. Massacres of Muslim civilians in 1990 and 1991 by Tamil militants, and retaliatory attacks by government-armed Muslim home guards on Tamil civilians further divided the two communities.

[2] Most "Indian," or "up-country" Tamils were brought to Sri Lanka from southern India by the British to work on tea plantations in the central highlands within the last 150 years. There are other "Indian" Tamils in Sri Lanka, such as the Chettis, who are the descendants of South Indian merchants, many of whom settled in Colombo.

nationalism.[3] Less than a decade after independence, the two groups were already deeply divided.

What began as a struggle for cultural affirmation, political representation, economic advancement and linguistic parity between Sinhala and Tamil, ended in communal riots and massacres. Anti-Tamil riots erupted in 1956 and 1958, in 1977, in August 1981, and reached a climax in July 1983, when officially promoted violence led to a civil war. In the course of the war, large-scale massacres of Muslim and Sinhalese civilians by Tamil militants, and Tamil civilians by army personnel and armed civilian defense units were frequent.

"Sinhala Only"

The first post-independence outbreak of ethnic rioting occurred in June 1956 after Parliament passed then Prime Minister S.W.R.D. Bandaranaike's Official Language Act (also referred to as the "Sinhala Only" act), which designated Sinhala as the sole official language of government administration and education. Tamil politicians organized peaceful demonstrations protesting the policy, which they viewed as discriminatory. In reaction to such protests, Sinhalese Buddhist partisans engaged in widespread anti-Tamil rioting.

Sinhalese nationalists who supported the "Sinhala Only" legislation saw it as redress to the injustice of an English-dominated system that suppressed the Sinhalese majority. But the Tamil minority, who had relied heavily on English, was put at a disadvantage. When the Tamil Federal Party, which had campaigned heavily against the bill, sponsored a general strike in Tamil-majority areas and held demonstrations in several communities, rioting erupted. In Colombo, Sinhalese rioters threw rocks through windows and looted stores. Over one hundred arrests were made and more than ninety people were injured. In the days that followed, rioting erupted in Trincomalee and Batticaloa, port towns in the Eastern Province, and at the site of the government-sponsored Gal Oya colonization scheme in Amparai District, where over one hundred Tamils were killed by Sinhalese settlers. The army was brought in to stop the violence, and two years of relative calm followed.

In May 1958, violence broke out again in conjunction with a meeting called by the Federal Party to decide whether to sponsor another civil disobedience campaign, this time in the northern town of Vavuniya, against the "Sinhala only" policy. Militant Sinhalese nationalists opposed the gathering, and their supporters stoned buses and trains carrying delegates to the meeting via the eastern town of

---

[3] K.M. De Silva, *A History of Sri Lanka* (New Delhi: 1981), p. 496.

Polonnaruwa. One train was derailed and its passengers were attacked and beaten; Tamil-owned houses and shops were burnt by Sinhalese laborers. As anti-Tamil rioting spread to Colombo, hundreds of Tamils were killed, and tens of thousands fled to refugee camps. Some 2,000 Sinhalese living in northern Sri Lanka also fled to camps to escape retaliation. The government was widely criticized for failing to act quickly to stem the violence. As two Sri Lankan academics described it,

> ...the country was aflame with riots and four days passed without the declaration of a state of emergency. Hundreds of innocent civilians were murdered. People were tortured, beaten and shot simply for not being able to pronounce certain words correctly; a number of *goondas* [thugs] killed their own people who were too frightened to pronounce words correctly. The government's lack of response would prove to be the rule rather than the exception, and Tamils, moderates and extremists, were infuriated.[4]

The government's handling of the 1958 riots radicalized a great many Tamils. Not only had the official response been slow, but when a public statement was made, it actually served to inflame anti-Tamil sentiment. And when the government finally did invoke emergency measures to calm the violence, the nonviolent Tamil Federal Party was banned, along with extreme Sinhalese nationalists who had advocated violence. Federal Party leaders were placed under house arrest.

In the wake of the violence, the Federal Party's demand for Tamil autonomy gained wide-spread support from the Tamil electorate, first as it proposed under a federalist constitution, and gradually, as this ambition was repeatedly frustrated, as an independent state under the banner of "Eelam."[5]

While Federal Party leaders were under house arrest from June to September 1958, Parliament finally passed legislation which permitted the "reasonable use of Tamil." It allowed Tamil in elementary education, correspondence with the government, local administration and civil service exams.

---

[4] Arul S. Aruliah and Anusha Aruliah, "The Evolution of Ethnic Conflict in Sri Lanka," *Refuge* (Ontario: Center for Refugee Studies, York University, June 1993) Volume 13, Number 3, p. 6.

[5] Eelam is the ancient Tamil name for the island of Sri Lanka and now refers to the independent Tamil homeland sought by secessionists.

But the legislation did not meet federalist demands for greater devolution of power.

In 1959, Prime Minister Bandaranaike was assassinated by a Buddhist monk who belonged to a radical Sinhalese faction, possibly because he attempted a compromise with the Tamil Federal Party over the language issue following the violence[6]. His widow, Sirimavo Bandaranaike, took over as head of the Sri Lanka Freedom Party (SLFP), won the presidential election in 1960 and signed provisions of the "Sinhala Only" Act which declared that Sinhala would be implemented as the language of administration by 1961. Protests launched by the Federal Party led for the first time to military suppression of civil disobedience in the North and East.

Mrs. Bandaranaike also instituted state control over government-assisted secondary schools, angering the Roman Catholic minority. The predominantly Christian military launched an unsuccessful coup attempt in 1962, but Mrs. Bandaranaike retained power and the country remained relatively peaceful through the election of the United National Party (UNP) government under Dudley Senanayake in 1965. In 1970 Mrs. Bandaranaike was returned to power under the banner of the United Front (UF), a coalition of opposition parties.

The Rise of Sinhalese and Tamil Insurgency

Within a year of Mrs. Bandaranaike's election, the government faced an armed insurgency by another communally defined political group: a radical youth organization called the Janatha Vimukti Peramuna (JVP) or People's Liberation Front. The JVP was founded by disaffected and underemployed Sinhalese youth, the first generation to be educated in Sinhala after the enactment of the Sinhala only legislation. The Sinhalese Marxist-nationalist JVP, which focussed on the interests of the Sinhalese peasantry, was both anti-Indian (it saw Indian economic expansion in Sri Lanka as a successor to British imperialism) and by extension anti-Tamil, as Tamils were thought to have political and cultural ties to south India. But the JVP's youth, guerrilla tactics, jungle training camps, and attacks on elite political leadership provided a model for young Tamil militants a decade later.[7]

---

[6] There are also allegations that he may have been the victim of a corruption scandal disguised as a political killing.

[7] Many thousands of suspected JVP supporters were killed and arrested in government counterinsurgency efforts in the 1970s. JVP prisoners taken at that time were subsequently pardoned and the organization began to participate in elections as a legal political party. It was banned again in 1983. The government-JVP conflict was primarily a political struggle, with both sides being predominately Sinhalese. It is therefore outside the scope of this report. We note, however, that after 1987 when the

In 1972, The United Front introduced a new Constitution that pushed many moderate Tamils further into Eelamist politics. The constitution (which changed the name of the country from the Dominion of Ceylon to the Republic of Sri Lanka, thereby severing the last official ties with Britain[8]) declared the country a Sinhala Buddhist republic and distinguished the rights of "citizens" from those of "persons" residing in Sri Lanka, radically restricting the latter. Tamils of Indian origin, who had been embraced by Sri Lankan Tamil politicians of this era under the umbrella of "Tamil-speaking people," were treated as stateless under the country's citizenship laws, and deprived of many rights. This combined with increasingly discriminatory university admission policies for Tamils led to protests in Jaffna.[9] By 1973, even mainstream Tamil political leaders, represented by a coalition party called the Tamil United Front, were convinced that Tamils could only gain full rights in a separate state in their "traditional homeland" of the North and East.[10]

JVP launched another major assault against the Sri Lankan government, tens of thousands of suspected JVP sympathizers were disappeared or killed in the ensuing government crackdown.

[8] As the Dominion of Ceylon, the country's highest court of judicial appeal was the Privy Council in London.

[9] Until 1970, entrance to universities in Sri Lanka had been based on academic achievement tested through competitive examinations. Largely because science facilities in Jaffna were good, Tamil students were represented in proportionately larger numbers in the sciences than their total numbers *vis-a-vis* other ethnic groups. In 1969-70, 35 percent of student admissions in the sciences, and 45 percent of students admitted to engineering and medical faculties were Tamil. After 1970, the system was changed so that Tamil students needed to obtain higher aggregate marks to enter universities in these fields. Quota systems and "other schemes were [also] introduced, all of them representing a departure from the practice of selecting students on the basis of actual marks obtained at an open competitive examination." *See*, K.M. De Silva, *Managing Ethnic Tensions in a Multi-Ethnic Society; Sri Lanka 1880-1985 (Lanham: 1986),* p. 262.

In 1975 the Tamil percentage of admissions into engineering and medical faculties had dropped to 14.1 percent and 17.4 percent respectively.

[10] The TUF's platform also demanded parity of status for Tamil with Sinhalese as an official language, the extension of citizenship rights to Indian Tamils, an official commitment to a secular state, and constitutional guarantees of universal fundamental

Mrs. Bandaranaike remained in office until 1977, her mandate extended by the new constitution and the state of emergency proclaimed in response to the JVP insurgency. She was succeeded by J.R. Jayawardene, who introduced yet another Constitution. In 1978, the Constitution of the Democratic Socialist Republic of Sri Lanka gave the country a French-style presidential system. The system increased executive power, and Jayawardene, then prime minister, became the first president.

Communal tension was high during the 1977 elections. The successor to the Tamil United Front, the Tamil United Liberation Front (TULF), with its promises of Eelam, won more than double the number of parliamentary seats as had the SLFP, and for the first time since independence a Tamil, A. Amirthalingam, was Leader of the Opposition. Meanwhile, militant Tamil youth from the North were organizing guerrilla groups with support from offices in Tamil Nadu, India. When they killed two Sinhalese policemen in Jaffna in mid-August 1977, anti-Tamil rioting broke out in many parts of the island. The violence lasted more than a month. Over one hundred people were killed and over 25,000 were displaced.[11]   Many Indian Tamils fled to the Eastern Province.

This time, the government did not declare a state of emergency to quell the violence. This failure to deploy official forces has been interpreted as an indication that the government could no longer trust the army and police to enforce the law.[12]   Criticism was levelled against the government for placing blame for the riots on Tamil politicians. Basing its conclusions on the findings of a presidential commission of inquiry into the riots of August and September 1977 (the Sansoni Commission), the government attributed the violence to the killings of the policemen in Jaffna, to inflammatory statements by Tamil leaders, and to Tamil separatist aspirations.[13]

From the Tamil point of view, the violence of the youths and the

---

rights and freedoms.

[11] *Managing Ethnic Tensions in Multi-Ethnic Societies*, p. 288.

[12] Ibid., pp. 325- 326.

[13] Virginia Leary, *Ethnic Conflict and Violence in Sri Lanka: Report of a Mission to Sri Lanka in July-August 1981 on behalf of the International Commission of Jurists, with a supplement by the ICJ staff for the period 1981-1983* (Geneva: August 1983), p. 20.

demand for separation were a consequence of increasing discrimination against them during the previous administration. The allegation that the violence was a reaction to the Tamil demand for a separate state [was] perceived as a threat that, if the Tamils persist[ed] in demanding separation, they [could] expect violence against them by the Sinhalese majority.[14]

Attacks by Tamil militants in the north on the security forces, and on political workers who supported the ruling party increased in the days leading up to local elections in June 1981. The killing of four police officers at an election rally on the eve of the elections led to further violence, culminating in the burning of the Jaffna library, one of Tamil Sri Lanka's most important cultural institutions.

According to both government and Tamil sources, a large group of police (estimated variously from 100-200) went on a rampage on the nights of May 31-June 1-2, burning the market area of Jaffna, the office of the Tamil newspaper, the home of V. Yogeswaran, Member of Parliament for Jaffna, and the Jaffna Public Library....According to government sources, the police, who had been brought to Jaffna from other parts of Sri Lanka, had mutinied and were uncontrollable....The 95,000 volumes of the Public Library destroyed by the fire included numerous culturally important and irreplaceable manuscripts.[15]

The burning of Jaffna library was the beginning of the end for many Jaffna Tamils, who saw the destruction wrought by government forces against such an important symbol of Tamil civil society to reflect a consistent pattern of discrimination against Tamils in Sri Lanka. In August 1981, anti-Tamil riots erupted again, beginning with a clash between Sinhalese and Tamil students at a sporting event in Amparai, and spreading to central Sri Lanka and Colombo. About ten Indian Tamils were killed and 5,000 fled to refugee camps. Unlike earlier ethnic riots, much of the violence appeared to be the work of organized gangs, with possible links to the government. Tamil observers complained that police and army personnel failed to intervene to stop attacks on Tamils until the government declared a state of emergency some two weeks after the violence

---

[14]Ibid.

[15] *Ethnic Conflict and Violence in Sri Lanka,* pp. 31- 31.

began.[16]

Despite recommendations by human rights organizations, including the International Commission of Jurists, the government failed to investigate and prosecute groups and individuals responsible for the 1981 violence; ethnic violence continued to escalate and repressive legislation was introduced and used almost exclusively against Tamils.[17]

The Road to Civil War

Two years later, organized violence against Tamils by ruling party politicians pushed Sri Lanka over the brink into civil war. On July 23, 1983, Tamil militants ambushed a patrol of soldiers near Jaffna, killing thirteen. The next day soldiers went on a rampage in Jaffna, killing forty-one people. Violence in Colombo broke out early in the morning on July 25. Rioting by organized gangs of Sinhalese paralyzed Colombo and quickly spread to other areas, claiming hundreds of lives, mostly Tamil, and destroying Tamil neighborhoods and businesses. In central Sri Lanka, nearly all Tamil-owned shops in the town of Nuwara Eliya were burnt, many with army-supplied gasoline, some by army personnel. Matale was devastated and a large portion of downtown Badulla was destroyed.[18]

In Colombo, police and soldiers stood by and watched as Tamils were attacked. In some cases they perpetrated the attacks themselves. The violence was well organized and politically supported. High ranking officials, including government ministers, were accused of orchestrating the violence.

In Kelaniya, Industries Minister Cyril Mathew's gangs were identified as the ones at work. The General Secretary of the government "union" the Jathika Sevaka Singamaya (J.S.S.) was

---

[16] Ibid., pp. 21- 22.

[17] In March 1982, the Prevention of Terrorism Act was made permanent and a new section 15A, was added to allow for detention in any place deemed appropriate by the arresting authority. In the early 1980s this act was used almost exclusively against Tamils. See, Leary, p. 92- 92.

[18] L. Piyadasa, *Sri Lanka: The Holocaust and After* (Marram Books, London: 1984), quoted in, Rajan Hoole, Daya Somasundaram, K. Sritharan, and Rajini Thiranagama, *The Broken Palmyra*, Vol. I, (Harvey Mudd College Press, Claremont, California: 1988), pp. 39- 40.

identified as the leader of gangs which wrought destruction and death all over Colombo and especially in Wellawatta, where as many as ten houses a street were destroyed. A particular UNP [United National Party] municipal councillor of the Dehiwela-Mount Lavinia Municipality led gangs in Mount Lavinia. In the Pettah (the bazaar area, where 442 shops were destroyed and murders were committed) the commander was the son of Aloysius Mudalali, the Prime Minister's right-hand man. And so on. Thugs who worked regularly for the leaders of the U.N.P., the Ministers of State and Party Headquarters, and in some cases uniformed military personnel and police, were seen leading the attack. They used vehicles of the Sri Lanka Transport Board (Minister in charge, M.H. Mohammed) and other government departments and state corporations. Trucks of the Ceylon Petroleum Corporations's oil refinery came from many miles away bringing the men who destroyed so much of Wellawatte.[19]

Tamil refugees poured into south India. Others fled to Tamil areas in the Northern and Eastern provices.

Then on July 25 and 27, 1983, fifty-three Tamil political detainees were massacred in Welikada Jail, a maximum security prison in Colombo. A magisterial inquiry returned a verdict of homicide, but despite the closed nature of the facility, no perpetrator was identified and there were no prosecutions.[20] Instead, the government banned three leftist parties, including the JVP, and passed the Sixth Amendment to the constitution which required all parliament members to swear an oath denouncing separatism. The TULF refused and Tamil areas lost their parliamentary representation.

When President Jayawardene finally made a public statement regarding the July 1983 riots four days later, he clearly showed his support for a Sinhalese majoritarianism which was not concerned with the plight of the Tamils. He did not condemn the violence against Tamils, but rather focused on violence perpetrated by the Tamil separatist movement. He announced that any organization that advocated separation would be banned, and referred to the anti-Tamil rioting as a "mass movement by the generality of the Sinhalese people," adding, "The time has

---

[19] Ibid., pp. 38- 39.

[20] In May 1994, nearly eleven years after the massacre, the government of Sri Lanka agreed to pay compensation to the families of the victims.

come to accede to the clamour and the national respect of the Sinhalese people."[21]

Tamil youth flocked to guerrilla organizations demanding an independent Tamil state. The largest of these was the Liberation Tigers of Tamil Eelam (LTTE), led by Velupillai Prabhakaran. As militant activity escalated, so did violence against civilians by both the guerrillas and by the Sri Lankan security forces. The war came to be characterized by massacres and reprisal killings of village populations—Tamil, Muslim and Sinhalese—by all parties, and by massive civilian displacement, including, during the second half of the war, the forced ejection of all Muslims, now considered a political liability by the LTTE, from militant-controlled areas of the North.

All parties treated civilians as military targets, and communal enmity as a tool to further military objectives. State forces, including soldiers, police and government-armed civilians militias, and Tamil secessionists committed grave violations of human rights and humanitarian law.

A policy of settling civilians in disputed areas to act as buffers in the conflict was pursued both by Tamil politicians and later by the Sri Lankan government. The history of Kent and Dollar farms near the town of Vavuniya, in northern Sri Lanka (an area now known as Weli Oya), provides a particularly vivid illustration of the way ethnic communities have been used to secure territory and send political messages.

The farms were originally donated by a wealthy Tamil landowner for the resettlement of plantation workers displaced by anti-Tamil violence in 1977. At this time many Tamil politicians were advocating the resettlement of Tamil refugees of Indian origin into areas that bordered Sinhalese-dominated regions to provide a buffer between the Sinhalese and Jaffna Tamils.

The farms were raided by the Vavuniya police in mid-1984. The police claimed they had driven away the Tamils who settled there because the settlers were terrorists. The government then took over the farms and settled them with Sinhalese ex-convicts as part of a program sponsored by then-National Security Minister Lalith Athulathmudali to help diffuse the "Tamil problem."

On November 30, 1984 the LTTE committed its first large-scale massacre of civilians, a night attack on the settlers of Kent and Dollar farms. At least seventy Sinhalese villagers were killed when LTTE fighters pulled families from their homes, bound their hands, and shot them in the heads, execution style. The LTTE claimed the settlers, who were former convicts, were armed. But the way in which the victims were killed clearly indicated there had been no gun battle, and some of

---

[21] S.J. Tambiah, *Ethnic Fratricide and the Dismantling of Democracy*, (University of Chicago Press, Chicago: 1986), p. 27.

the dead were children.

The government resettled thousands of former prisoners, Sinhalese fishing families, retired military personnel and families displaced by the huge Mahavelli water project into the north and east. By 1985, state resources were used to move more than 50,000 Sinhalese into traditionally Tamil areas like Trincomalee, Vavuniya and Mullaitivu. These settlements also created buffers between Tamil and Sinhalese districts, and provided communal barriers between Jaffna and the Tamil villages of the Eastern province. Needless to say, these communities proved extremely vulnerable to attack, leading the government to arm residents known as "home guards" to protect them. By 1987, there were an estimated 11,000 armed home guards in the Northern and Eastern provinces. These home guards participated in a number of extrajudicial executions and massacres, sometimes acting independently, at other times operating in conjunction with military personnel.

In Mannar district on December 4, 1984 some 107 civilians, including local residents and bus passengers were massacred after an army jeep was attacked by Tamil militants and a soldier killed. Similar attacks continued throughout 1985.

Tamil militants also continued to engage in massacres of civilians. One of the largest occurred on May 14, 1985 when a group of Tamil militants dressed in army uniforms captured a bus and drove it into the bus station in Anuradhapura, the ancient Sinhala Buddhist capital. Once in Anuradhapura, they opened fire with automatic weapons, shooting pedestrians as they made their way to the sacred *bo* tree[22], one of the holiest Buddhist shrines in Sri Lanka. In all, 146 Buddhist pilgrims and other civilians were killed. The massacre was apparently in retaliation for an earlier killing of forty-three Tamil civilians by Sri Lankan military at Valvetithurai.

Initially, a small militant organization, the Eelam Revolutionary Organization of Students (EROS) claimed responsibility for the massacre, but it later retracted the statement, and joined the People's Liberation Organization for Tamil Eelam (PLOTE) in denouncing the incident. The groups accused the LTTE.[23]

---

[22] Sri Lanka's bo tree is believed to be a branch of the tree under which the Buddha attained enlightenment in India.

[23] Besides the LTTE, EROS and PLOTE, other Tamil militant groups active during this period were the Eelam People's Revolutionary Liberation Front (EPRLF) and its offshoot the Eelam National Democratic Liberation Front (ENDLF), and TELO, the Tamil Eelam Liberation Organization. In May 1986 the LTTE began systematically eliminating rival militant groups. Hundreds of people were killed in internecine fighting

The role of the state and of guerrilla forces in fomenting communal violence was even clearer in their manipulation of the relationship between Sri Lanka's Tamil and Muslim communities. Tamil politicians had long sought to include both Indian Tamils and Muslims under the umbrella of Tamil-speaking people, a move that would have greatly increased their constituency. The town of Trincomalee, for example had nearly equal numbers of Tamils, Muslims and Sinhalese in 1981. Amparai district's population was only 20 percent Tamil, but over 41 percent Muslim. For a time the attempts to join forces appeared successful. In fact, early on many Muslim youths were active supporters of Tamil militants groups like the LTTE. But other Muslims distrusted pro-Eelam politics, which they felt did not adequately address Muslim needs, and formed new alliances that Tamil militants feared would give the government more influence in the East.

Government forces capitalized on Tamil-Muslim differences as a means to weaken the militant movement, sometimes seeming openly to support Muslim violence against Tamils. In turn, the LTTE treated Muslim politicians as traitors and sponsored attacks on Muslim civilians. As civilians became military targets, massacres were employed to move them out of strategic territory; communal enmity was promoted to prevent the development of political coalitions that might weaken the hold of either party to the conflict.[24]

In Batticaloa and Amparai districts in 1985 and again in 1990, witnesses reported seeing members of the security forces in the vicinity during attacks on Tamil communities which resulted in many homes being burned, and deaths of Tamils and Muslims killed in reprisal attacks. While it was evident that official forces were aware of the attacks, no effort was made to stop them.

Indo-Sri Lanka Accord of 1987
During the 1980s, the LTTE and other Tamil organizations maintained offices in India and the Indian government appeared sympathetic to Tamil claims, even going so far as to air-drop relief supplies after the Sri Lankan military launched an offensive on the Jaffna peninsula. But India was not interested in sponsoring separatism. Rather, Indian policy seemed designed to keep political pressure on the Sri Lankan government to discourage its increasingly pro-Western foreign policy and to encourage dialogue between the Sri Lankan government and

---

and representatives of these other groups fled to India.

[24] Kenneth Bush, "Reading Between the Lines: Intra-Group Heterogeneity and Conflict in Sri Lanka," *Refuge* (Ottawa: Center for Refugee Studies, York University, June 1993), Volume 13, Number 3, p. 18.

Tamil militants.

The Sri Lankan government entered into negotiations with India and on July 27, 1987 the two countries signed the Indo-Sri Lanka Accord. The agreement made Tamil a national language alongside Sinhala, and established Provincial Councils to address Tamil grievances. The Northern and Eastern Provinces were merged, pending a referendum in the East scheduled for 1988, but not yet held. In return, Tamil militants were ordered to surrender their arms. At the request of President Jayawardene, Indian peace keeping forces were deployed in the Northern and Eastern Provinces. The LTTE opposed the accord, refused to disarm, launched a campaign to eliminate rival Tamil groups, and again began attacking Sinhalese civilians. Sinhalese groups, particularly the SLFP and the JVP also objected to the agreement because they saw it as pro-Tamil. Rioting erupted again in the south.

By September 1987, the Indian government had stationed 7,000 soldiers and 1,000 of its Central Reserve Police Force (CRPF) commandos in Sri Lanka. As operations against the LTTE intensified the number of Indian troops in Sri Lanka rose to 20,000. The Indian Peace Keeping Forces (IPKF), ostensibly sent in to disarm the LTTE and other militants, stop the carnage against the Tamils and end the war proved to be abusive and unpopular. They also engaged in attacks on civilians and made their own contribution to continuing instability by supporting a rival Tamil faction, the Eelam People's Revolutionary Liberation Front (EPRLF) against the LTTE.

On September 26, LTTE political leader Amirthalingam Thileepan died, having undertaken a fast unto death protesting implementation of the accord. Demonstrations erupted throughout the north and east. After India and the LTTE reached an agreement to nominate a majority of LTTE candidates to an interim council of the north and east, violent attacks began on Sinhalese in the East.

By the end of the first week of October some 200 Sinhalese had been killed in rioting and in attacks by the LTTE and many more were missing. Some 20,000 fled to Sinhalese areas of the country. As we reported in 1987:

> By October 1, what had appeared to be (and in part was) a spontaneous communal clash took on the appearance of an organized pogrom, with LTTE members taking the lead is a seeming effort to drive Sinhalese out of the Eastern Province. For the next few days young men on motorcycles with guns warned Sinhalese to leave if they wanted to save their lives, then returned later to burn houses, destroy gardens, and kill those

who resisted.[25]

The LTTE undertook a similar campaign in October 1990. After a series of massacres of hundreds of Muslim villagers in eastern Sri Lanka in August and September 1990, LTTE fighters informed heads of Muslim villages in the northern districts of Mannar, Mullaitivu, Kilonochchi and Jaffna that residents had days or sometimes only hours to vacate the area or face a similar fate. Some 40,000 northern Muslims fled to the coast where Muslim-owned fishing boats ferried them over rough seas to make-shift refugee camps in Puttalam district. Others travelled as far south as Colombo with little hope of returning to their villages. By September 1992, an estimated 150,000 northern Muslims were displaced.

Opposition to the presence of the Indian troops mounted in the south, and in April 1989, the Sri Lankan government entered negotiations with the LTTE. By June, they had declared a ceasefire with government security forces. Fighting continued, however, between the LTTE and IPKF. By July, both the LTTE and the Sri Lankan government had demanded the withdrawal of Indian troops. In September, the Indian Government agreed to withdraw its troops, and by the end of 1989 the IPKF had withdrawn from all but two northeastern districts, Trincomalee and Jaffna and the LTTE began to take over primary responsibility for policing the Northeast Province.[26] They collected taxes, established checkpoints, and systematically exterminated members of rival Tamil groups who had been supported by the Indian army.

In March 1990, the last Indian troops finally left Sri Lanka. Most of the EPRLF leadership fled the northeast as a result, fearing an LTTE backlash with some justification: several EPRLF leaders were subsequently assassinated by suspected LTTE members. Following a brief respite fighting resumed in June 1990 when LTTE guerrillas broke the fourteen-month ceasefire with the Sri Lankan government and attacked a military convoy in Vavuniya. This was the first in a series of escalating attacks against police and military personnel which killed

---

[25] Asia Watch, *Cycles of Violence* (Washington, DC: Human Rights Watch, 1987), p. 51.

[26] In December 1988 the Northern and Eastern provinces were merged into the Northeastern Province as provided by the Indo-Sri Lanka Accord of July 1987. This merger is subject to approval by the electorate of the three districts formerly comprising the Eastern Province, but a referendum has not been held. Human Rights Watch/Asia refers to this area as the "northeast" (rather than "north and east") because of its current legal status; we take no position on what this area's future status should be.

hundreds and effectively ended negotiations between the LTTE and the Sri Lankan government. Within a week the government had once again declared war on the LTTE.

Since 1990, thousands of Tamil civilians have been killed and disappeared by government forces, including members of home guard units. Hundreds of Muslim and Sinhalese villagers have been killed by Tamil militants. Most of these incidents have not been investigated, and even in the few well publicized cases where an investigation has been launched, prosecutions have not followed, or disciplinary action has not been made public.

In 1994 the war continued unabated, although the mass killings of ethnic populations that characterized fighting in 1990 and 1991 had declined significantly. Over one million people were at least temporarily displaced during the course of the conflict, and about half that number remained so. Muslim civilians ejected from northern Sri Lanka by the LTTE in 1990 are still housed in temporary camps, mainly in Puttalam district on the western coast.

Political violence in southern Sri Lanka reached a climax in 1993 with the assassinations of President Ranasinghe Premadasa and his chief political opponent, Lalith Athulathmudali, within days of each other. Athulathmudali, who had himself spearheaded an abusive military campaign against Tamil militants as government security minister in the 1980s, was shot and killed during a campaign rally in late April. President Premadasa was killed on May 1 by a suicide bomber thought to be a member of the LTTE. During the investigations that followed, police conducted large-scale detentions of Tamil civilians.

Police in Colombo, Kandy and other urban areas continued to target Tamils systematically for arbitrary arrests and detention throughout 1994, afterwards detentions decreased but did not cease entirely. Between June 1993 and December 1994 thousands of Tamils were picked up for questioning. These arrests were made almost entirely on the basis of ethnicity, and reports of mistreatment in detention were common.

The assassinations weakened the UNP's seventeen-year hold on power. In an August 1994 parliamentary election, a newly formed coalition party called the People's Alliance (PA), headed by Chandrika Kumaratunge (daughter of former Prime Minister Srimavo Bandaranaike) ousted the UNP. The PA won on a campaign platform that promised a negotiated settlement of the civil war and increased accountability for past human rights violations.[27]

---

[27] Kumaratunge was named prime minister, but then ran and won in the presidential election of December 1994, and appointed her mother prime minister. In October her campaign was marred by another assassination bombing that killed

Expanding on initiatives begun by the Premadasa regime to combat international criticism of its human rights record, the PA mandated governmental human rights bodies to review detentions made under special security laws and to investigate the tens of thousands of disappearances reported to have occurred after 1988. While welcoming the move, many human rights activists have criticized this initiative as incomplete since it fails to take into account a large number of reported disappearances of Tamils after the civil war erupted in 1983. They also note the importance not only of discovering the fate of the missing, but also of identifying and prosecuting the perpetrators.

The LTTE and the Sri Lankan government entered into the first round of negotiations in October 1994. By January 1995 the two parties had agreed to a cease-fire and a partial lifting of a government-imposed economic embargo against the north. But to date negotiations have focused on reconstruction of the LTTE's war-ravaged territory and on the opening of land routes to allow civilians to travel south. No proposed political solution has yet been put forward.

Conclusion

By playing on communal sympathies to gain support from their constituencies, political forces in Sri Lanka aggravated ethnic discord, leading to widespread anti-Tamil riots. The politicization of the police and military along ethnic lines, the active involvement of government forces in ethnic attacks, and its failure to prosecute offenders for human rights violations against Tamil civilians, led to a rise in Tamil militancy and to attacks on Sinhalese and Muslim civilians. Government forces engaged in similar attacks on Tamils. Ethnic hatred escalated into civil war, a political conflict defined along ethnic lines. New efforts by Sri Lanka's government to redress the grievances of its citizens and account for the abuses which have been committed against members of all ethnic groups by state forces and other political actors is an essential first step in the creation of any lasting peace in Sri Lanka. But the damage done by years of politically contrived enmity and bloodshed promises to make any peace process a tentative one, and any political solution, fragile. The Sri Lankan people have shown great popular support for an end to the fighting, but it will take a lot to repair their faith in political forces.

Kumaratunga's chief political opponent, UNP candidate Gamini Dissanayake and fifty-three others. An LTTE suicide bomber was suspected to have carried out the bombing, although the LTTE denied responsibility.

KENYA

In late 1991, concerted domestic and international pressure for political liberalization and respect for human rights forced the repressive government of President Daniel arap Moi to repeal a 1982 constitutional amendment and legalize a multiparty system. In August 1991, an internal democracy movement demanded an end to the monopoly on power held by the Kenya African National Union (KANU), which had led Kenya since independence in 1963. President Moi, however, claimed that the return of his country to multiparty rule would threaten the stability of the state by polarizing the country along ethnic lines. By the time multiparty elections were held at the end of 1992, it appeared that his claim was accurate: Kenya's political parties had divided largely along ethnic lines, while "tribal clashes" in the rural areas of western Kenya had left hundreds dead and tens of thousands displaced. It seemed that Kenya, previously an example of relative stability in the region, was at risk of sliding into a low-level civil war.

The Moi government capitalized on unaddressed land ownership and tenure issues, dating back to the colonial period, between those pastoral ethnic groups who were originally ousted from the Rift Valley area by the British and subsequent squatter labor which settled on the land following independence. The clashes drew on these competing claims in order to inflame violence among certain ethnic groups. The great majority of the victims came from the ethnic groups associated with the political opposition. By late 1993, Human Rights Watch/Africa estimated that 1,500 people had died in the clashes and approximately 300,000 were displaced. Despite Moi's pronouncements, however, the violence was not a spontaneous reaction to the reintroduction of multiparty politics. Although ethnicity has been crucial in the politics of the Kenyan state and was central to the development of the clashes, it was not the motor force behind the outbreak of violence: the clashes were deliberately instigated and manipulated by KANU politicians anxious to retain their hold on power in the face of mounting internal and external pressure for change in government. Despite a series of damning reports, including an exhaustive document prepared by a parliamentary committee, those who were alleged to be directing the violence and the attackers themselves enjoyed legal and political impunity for their acts. Human rights abuses instigated or condoned by the state were central to the outbreak and the continuation of violence.

Since the election, the frequency of the large scale "ethnic" attacks has diminished steadily, but, periodic incidents continue. While a resettlement program has been instituted, with the joint backing of the Kenyan government and the United Nations Development Program (UNDP), the majority of the displaced victims are unable to return to their farms safely. Moreover, the government continues systematically to harass displaced victims and relief officials involved with feeding the displaced.

The government's motive for instigating the violence appears multifold: first, to prove its assertion that multiparty politics would lead to tribal chaos; second, to punish ethnic groups that are perceived to support the political opposition, namely the Kikuyu, Luo and Luhya; third, to terrorize and intimidate non-Kalenjins and non-Maasais to leave the Rift Valley Province, one of Kenya's most fertile farming areas, and to allow Kalenjins and Maasai to take over the land. Finally, the violence plays a part in renewed calls by Kalenjin and Maasai politicians for the introduction of *majimboism*, a federal system based on ethnicity. A majimbo system would mandate that only members of those pastoral groups originally on the land before colonialism such as the Kalenjin and Maasai would have political and economic power in the Rift Valley Province, which has the largest number of parliamentary seats and is the base of Kenya's agricultural economy.

Background

British colonization of the area that is now Kenya caused a major disruption of existing landholding patterns, due to the large influx of white settlers. A succession of land regulations between 1899 and 1915 expropriated much of the best land for the use of European farmers, and restricted Africans to "native reserves" a fraction of the size of the land they had previously occupied. Largely pastoralist groups, such as the Maasai and the various sub-groups of the Kalenjin, were prevented from using their traditional grazing grounds (regarded by the whites as "undeveloped"); cultivators, such as the Kikuyu, were restricted to areas too small to sustain the subdivisions of land as population grew.[1] However, in the

---

[1] The Kalenjin are made up of a number of smaller groups speaking Nilotic languages and sharing similar cultural traditions. Together they form about 11 percent of the Kenyan population. In precolonial times, the Kalenjin were largely pastoralist and the various subgroups had few political links; the sense of common "Kalenjin" identity was born as a result of British colonial policies and has strengthened since independence. President Moi is a Kalenjin. The Kikuyu, the largest ethnic group in Kenya, were before colonization already a more homogeneous ethnicity, speaking a Bantu language related to those spoken throughout a wide area of eastern and southern Africa, and cultivating the area spreading north from what is now Nairobi towards Mount Kenya, although they were not grouped under one political authority. They were the group most immediately and drastically impacted by colonization, both by the alienation of their land and also in gaining the most rapid access to education and thus political influence. The Maasai, much romanticized in British colonial writings, were Nilotic-speaking pastoralists

early years of white settlement the weak commercial position of the settlers led to an influx of a large number of African "squatters" into white areas. In a system known as "kaffir farming," these share croppers were granted land and permission to cultivate on their own account in return for working for set periods for the nominal owner of the land. Although several ethnic groups were represented among the squatters, it was overwhelmingly landless Kikuyu from the overcrowded reserves in Central Province that took this opportunity, thus obtaining land for cultivation on relatively easy terms and establishing communities parallel to the settler economy. European farmers gained otherwise unobtainable labor for their own uses.[2]

As the colonial state strengthened and European farmers became more successful, new restrictions were placed on squatters' freedom to cultivate on their own account. In an attempt to create a purely wage economy, severe limits were placed on the amount of land that could legally be cultivated by each squatter family, and on the amount of stock they could hold. Increasing discontent at these and other repressive measures, coupled with the issue of land alienation more generally, led to the rise in the 1950s of the armed resistance movement known as Mau Mau, recruited predominantly from the Kikuyu squatter population. A cross-tribal elite African nationalist movement, the Kenya African Union (KAU), which was formed in 1944, also demanded African access to land in the "white highlands." In 1953, KAU was banned and its president, Jomo Kenyatta, imprisoned. Mau Mau was crushed by the harsh enforcement of emergency laws.[3] Despite efforts during the last years of colonial rule to make more land available to squatters and create a class of richer peasant farmers with security of tenure, the

---

originally grazing their animals over a wide area and later restricted to a reserve along the border with Tanganyika (Tanzania). The division between "pastoralist" and "cultivator" is, however, a generalization: most groups practiced a mixed agriculture.

[2] See, for example, Tabitha Kanogo, *Squatters and Roots of Mau Mau 1905 - 1963* (Nairobi: Heinemann Kenya Ltd, 1987).

[3] Mau Mau took the form of an internal Kikuyu civil war as well as a challenge to colonial authority. By the end of 1956, when Mau Mau had been overcome, only thirty-two European civilians, but approximately 13,000 Africans, nearly 2,000 of them civilians and mainly Kikuyu, had died in the conflict.

land hunger of the squatters remained.[4]

In 1960, the state of emergency was revoked and substantial African representation in the national legislative council was allowed for the first time, in preparation for a transition to self-rule and independence. African political parties were legalized, and though Kenyatta was still in prison, KANU was established by the former leaders of KAU. As independence approached, the competing interests of the intellectual elite of KANU, the militant and largely Kikuyu squatter population and the minority pastoral and agricultural groups resulted in serious divisions within the African political leadership. These divisions were exploited by the white colonial government and settler population, who feared KANU's commitment to the redistribution of land. The Kenya African Democratic Union (KADU), of which future President Moi was a leader, was also formed. KADU, which had significant settler support, was a party of ethnic minorities such as the Kalenjin, Luhya and Maasai, who claimed original use of the "white highlands" and feared a centralized government controlled by the larger agricultural groups, especially the Luo and Kikuyu who dominated KANU.[5]

KADU pursued a political philosophy of regionalism, majimboism in Kiswahili, which would allow semi-autonomous regions, based on ethnicity, to have substantial decision-making power. The central government, in turn, would have limited and defined federal role. They viewed majimboism as the only political option to safeguard the rights of the minority groups. The British settler population were quick to provide KADU with financial support in a bid to counter support for KANU, which was identified with strong nationalistic interest. Eventually, KANU won a pre-independence election with a decisive majority resulting in a compromise in which British settler interests were safeguarded. Soon after, Kenya became a *de facto* one-party state, following the voluntary dissolution of KADU and another party, the African People's Party.

---

[4] In 1955, the "Swynnerton Plan" (*A Plan to Intensify the Development of African Agriculture in Kenya*, compiled by R.J.M. Swynnerton, Nairobi: Government Printer, 1955), provided for a program of consolidation of holdings, with the aim of creating an "African middle class: that would provide a buffer between the militant and landless peasants of Mau Mau and the white settler population."

[5] Like the Kalenjin, the Luhyas, who live generally in the west of Kenya towards Uganda, are made up of several smaller ethnic groups, the collective description also dating from the colonial period. The Luo, speaking a Nilotic language closer to the languages of the Kalenjin than that of the Bantu Kikuyu, live mostly in the region abutting Lake Victoria.

The independence settlement and subsequent dissolution of all parties but KANU created a government which was nominally a multiethnic alliance—in which Moi, himself a Kalenjin leader of KADU, became vice-president in 1967. KANU rule under Kenyatta was characterized by strong Kikuyu nationalist sentiments. In 1969, Kenyatta banned attempts by Luo opposition leader Oginga to form a second party. The move was seen by many Kenyans not only as a means of ensuring the preeminence of KANU, but also that of the Kikuyu.

Moreover, the land issue was never fully addressed. British settler interests were safeguarded, while no effort was made to deal with the competing claims of those pastoral ethnic groups who originally were ousted from the Rift Valley area by the British and subsequently the squatter laborers who settled on the land. Moreover, population growth further increased the pressure on land.[6] British settlers were given the option to retain the land they had expropriated through colonialism. Consequently, large tracts of some of the best farmland in Kenya remain the owned by British settlers. For those settlers who wanted to sell their land, a land settlement scheme was set up with the newly independent government to assist the former squatter labor to buy land either individually or through collective schemes.

Among the Kikuyu, unlike communal pastoral groups such as the Maasai and Kalenjin, farming was an established practice. Accordingly, many Kikuyus were eager to take advantage of the opportunity to purchase land. Encouraged and assisted by President Kenyatta, large numbers of Kikuyus bought land in the Rift Valley in the 1960s and 1970s and moved from the overcrowded Central Province. These farms have been at the center of the recent ethnic violence.

When Kenyatta died in 1978, Vice-President Moi succeeded him as president, over the opposition of the Kikuyu elite. As Kenyatta had used political power to give disproportionate benefits to his own Kikuyu ethnic group, so Moi did for the minority Kalenjin. Kalenjin and members of allied groups such as the Maasai were appointed to key positions within the national government and came to dominate administrative positions at local and regional levels. In 1982, to forestall the registration of a new party by politicians discontented with the

---

[6] Kenya's population density, estimated at 44 percent per square kilometers, is twice the average for sub-Saharan Africa. Moreover, approximately 75 percent of the population is contained in only 10 percent of the land area, where rainfall is highest and land most fertile. Population growth, at 3.5 percent is amongst the highest rates in the world. Human Development Report 1994, New York/Oxford: UNDP/Oxford University Press, 1994, *Africa South of the Sahara 1991* (Twentieth Edition), (London: Europa Publications, 1990).

increasing severity of his rule, the constitution was amended to make Kenya a *de jure* one-party state. An abortive coup attempt several months later was followed by a crackdown on all potential opponents.

By 1990, repression had provoked a vigorous movement in support of a multiparty system.[7] On July 7, 1990, thousands of people gathered at a pro-democracy rally outside Nairobi: confrontations with security police led to three days of rioting, known as the Saba Saba riots,[8] in which at least twenty, and probably many more, died. In August 1991, a coalition calling itself the Forum for the Restoration of Democracy (FORD) was formed by prominent leaders of the political opposition - some of them colleagues of Kenyatta in the struggle for independence, others part of a new generation of young reformers—to demand the legalization of a multiparty system. At least partly in response to their demands, the consultative group of bilateral donors to Kenya suspended over US$1 billion of balance of payments support and other aid in November 1991, on economic, governance and human rights grounds. One month later, in December 1991, article 2(a) of the Kenyan constitution, outlawing opposition parties, was repealed.

As the campaign for multiparty democracy gained strength and then developed into a full election campaign, violence broke out between different ethnic groups, particularly in Rift Valley, Western and Nyanza provinces, the heart of the "white highlands" during colonial times. The "tribal clashes," as they became known, first broke out in October 1991, on the border of the three provinces , and rapidly spread to neighboring districts: bands of armed "Kalenjin warriors" attacked farms belonging to the Luo, Kikuyu or Luhya, the groups from which FORD drew its main support, destroying homes and driving the occupants away or killing those who resisted. By December 1991, when Parliament repealed the section of the constitution making Kenya a one-party state, large areas of the west of Kenya had been affected as tens of thousands were displaced from their land.

Although it seemed that the first outbreak of fighting was a simple land dispute between members of the Luo and Nandi groups (the Nandi are one of the Kalenjin subgroups), the violence rapidly took on the content and ethnic

---

[7] In 1986, an earlier movement know as MwaKenya had formed a somewhat diffuse locus of opposition to Moi from a wide spectrum of political and regional backgrounds. By early 1987 more than a hundred people had been detained in connection with the "conspiracy," some of them receiving lengthy terms of imprisonment.

[8] Saba Saba means "seven seven" (July 7) in Kiswahili.

breakdown of the wider political debate. FORD, the leader of the call for multipartyism, was dominated by Kikuyu, Luo and, to a lesser extent, Luhya at both leadership and grassroots levels. Although the coalition included members of other ethnic groups and based its political platform on the misuse of power by President Moi, it built much of its appeal on the resentment of its supporters at the domination of the government by Moi's own ethnic group, the Kalenjin, and its allies the Maasai. Moi, for his part, portrayed the call for multipartyism as an anti-Kalenjin movement and played on the fears of the minority ethnicities at the return to power of the economically dominant Kikuyu. At the same time, he argued that Kenya's multiethnic nature meant that multiparty politics would inevitably break down along ethnic lines, and that those divisions would inevitably lead to violence.

Kalenjin and Maasai politicians opportunistically revived the idea of majimboism championed by KADU at independence. In the name of regional self-government, they called for "non-indigenous" groups to leave the Rift Valley; that is, the descendants of those who had originally come to the Rift Valley only during colonial times. At a rally held in September 1991, soon before the first clashes broke out, Kalenjin MP Joseph Misoi read a statement declaring that a majimbo constitution had been drafted that would be tabled before the house if the proponents of multipartyism continued their efforts. Under this constitution,"outsiders" in the Rift Valley would be required to go back to their "motherland."[9] Other majimbo rallies called for the "true" Rift Valley residents to defend themselves from opposition plots to eliminate the indigenous peoples of the valley. At Meteitei Farm, where the first clashes had occurred, leaflets signed by a group calling itself the Nandi Warriors warned Luos to leave the area by December 12, 1991 or "face the consequences."[10]

Violence escalated during 1992, as the opposition mobilized for the election. The clashes decreased in intensity somewhat towards the end of the year, when international attention focused on the country during the lead-up to the elections, which were finally held on December 29, 1992. Despite the hopes of

---

[9] *Republic of Kenya Report of the Parliamentary Select Committee to Investigate the Ethnic Clashes in Western and other parts of Kenya* (Nairobi: Government Printer, September 1992), pp. 8-9.

[10] Human Rights Watch/Africa, *Divide and Rule: State-Sponsored Ethnic Violence in Kenya* (New York: Human Rights Watch, November 1993), p. 19.

many Kenyans for an end to Moi's rule, KANU was returned to power.[11] The KANU victory was based on only 36 percent of the popular vote and owed much to the division - largely along ethnic lines—of FORD into two parties, FORD-Kenya and FORD-Asili ("Original" FORD), to which was added a breakaway group from KANU, the Democratic Party.[12]

Many expected that the clashes would cease after Moi's election victory, but although some areas have been restored to calm, sporadic outbreaks of violence have continued. Throughout 1993 and 1994, large organized attacks by Kalenjin "warriors" occurred periodically. In November 1993, Human Rights Watch/Africa published a report on the "ethnic clashes" which estimated that the violence had by that date left at least 1,500 dead and as many as 300,000 internally displaced.[13] In some areas, residents who returned to their farms after being driven off were attacked a second or even third time. In March and September 1994, violent clashes broke out yet again in the Burnt Forest and Malo areas respectively.

While the large-scale attacks which characterized the pre-election violence have decreased, acts of intimidation and harassment aimed at individuals who attempt to return to their land continue. These reports of threats or actual violence have deterred the bulk of the estimated 300,000 displaced from returning. Most clash victims have congregated in large numbers at church compounds or abandoned buildings throughout Western, Nyanza and Rift Valley provinces. They live in destitute overcrowded conditions, some of them since the clashes first began over three years ago. To date, thousands of displaced victims have to farm on their land in the day and sleep elsewhere at night for fear of recurring attack. In many cases, displaced victims have found their land illegally occupied by Kalenjins or

---

[11] Although there were widespread allegations of irregularities in the conduct of the poll, international observers concluded that "[d]espite the fact that the whole electoral process cannot be given an unqualified rating as free and fair...we believe that the results in many instances directly reflect, however imperfectly, the will of the people. *The Presidential, Parliamentary and Civic elections in Kenya: The Report of the Commonwealth Observer Group* (London: Commonwealth Secretariat, 1993), p.40.

[12] FORD-K remained relatively multiethnic, but was dominated by Luos, Luhyas and members of some smaller groups. Later in 1993, further fault lines developed within the party between the Luo and other leaders. FORD-Asili and DP were both seen as Kikuyu parties, divided along regional lines.

[13] Human Rights Watch/Africa, *Divide and Rule.*

Maasais.[14]

Displaced victims have also been harassed by Kenyan government authorities. On several occasions, local government authorities have forcibly dispersed camps of displaced victims which have attracted media attention. In June 1993, government officials cleared a camp of displaced persons' Luhvas and Tesos at Endebess in Trans Nzoia district who had fled an attack by Kalenjins in December 1991. In January 1994, the government demolished the makeshift shacks at the displaced camp of Maela and closed down a medical clinic and a makeshift school at the camp. Approximately 30,000 people, predominantly Kikuyus, had initially sought refuge at Maela in October 1993 after being attacked by approximately 500 Maasais. In December 1994, government officials razed Maela camp and forcibly transported approximately 2,000 of the camp residents to Central Province (Kikuyu heartland). Families were separated and the camp residents were not told where they were being taken. The displaced Kikuyus who were taken to Central Province were questioned about their ethnicity and ancestral background and some were forcibly moved yet again. The government has begun to insist on the dispersal of other displaced camps in Rift Valley Province without providing alternative accommodation or assistance.

The Role of the Government in "Tribal Clashes"

Although the rise of the violence was clearly linked to the emergence of multipartyism and drew on longstanding tensions between Kenya's different ethnic groups, evidence rapidly emerged that the clashes of late 1991 and after, far from being the spontaneous reaction to competition among parties divided along ethnic lines, were being deliberately provoked by elements within the government. Soon after the clashes first erupted, rumors of the involvement of government ministers and officials in the violence began to circulate. More systematic investigations followed. In April 1992, the National Council of Churches of Kenya (NCCK), the coalition of Protestant churches which was heavily involved in providing relief to the victims, issued a report that linked the violence to high-ranking government officials. It concluded: "These clashes were and are politically motivated...to achieve through violence what was not achieved in the political platform, i.e. forcing majimboism on the Kenyan people. Here the strategy being to create a situation on the ground for a possible future political bargain in the debate about

---

[14]Human Rights Watch/Africa, *Multipartism Betrayed in Kenya: Continuing Rural Violence & Restrictions on Freedom of Speech and Assembly*, p. 13.

the system of government in future Kenya."[15] A further report issued by a coalition of groups in June 1992 stated that the attacks were organized under central command, often in the presence of local administration and security officers and that warriors who were arrested were often released unconditionally.[16]

Mounting pressure from opposition and church groups eventually forced President Moi to authorize an official investigation into the clashes. In September 1992, the parliamentary select committee appointed for this task delivered a sharply critical report confirming many of the earlier allegations, with all the more force because the committee, since it was formed before the elections, was made up only of KANU members. Besides stating that at least 779 had been killed and 56,000 families displaced by the violence, the report concluded that the attacks had been orchestrated by Kalenjin and Maasai politicians close to the president, including Vice-President George Saitoti and MPs Nicholas Biwott and Ezekiel Barng'etuny.[17] The Kiliku report, as it came to be known after the name of the chair of the committee, J. Kennedy Kiliku, cited evidence that the "Kalenjin warriors" carrying out the attacks had been paid by these officials for each person killed or house burnt down, and that government vehicles had transported the warriors to and from clash areas. The report recommended, *inter alia*, that "appropriate action be taken against those administration officials who directly or indirectly participated or encouraged the clashes."[18] The report was not adopted by the compliant KANU parliament, and no effort was made by the government to implement its recommendations. In April 1993, a further report was published by a group originally set up to monitor the conduct of the elections, which confirmed previous conclusions and updated the information to include violence since the election.[19]

---

[15] *The Cursed Arrow: Organized Violence Against Democracy in Kenya* (Nairobi: NCCK, April 1992), p. 1.

[16] *Interparties Symposium I Task Force Report*, Nairobi, June 11, 1992.

[17] Biwott, formerly Minister of Energy, had also been implicated in the 1990 murder of prominent Luo politician, Minister for Foreign Affairs Robert Ouko.

[18] *Report of the Parliamentary Select Committee to Investigate Ethnic Clashes in Western and Other Parts of Kenya* (Republic of Kenya: Government Printer, September 1992), p. 82.

[19] *Courting Disaster: A Report On The Continuing Terror, Violence And Destruction in the Rift Valley, Nyanza and Western Provinces of Kenya* (Nairobi: National Election Monitoring Unit (NEMU), April 29, 1993).

Investigations carried out by Human Rights Watch/Africa during 1993, which included extensive eyewitness interviews, supported the conclusion that the violence had been orchestrated and planned. Eyewitness reports of the violence were remarkably similar. Farms occupied by members of the Luo, Kikuyu or Luhya ethnic groups were attacked by groups of "Kalenjin warriors" coming from one or other of the subgroups of the Kalenjin ethnic group. Non-Kalenjin houses were burnt and their owners driven away. The attackers were often dressed in an informal uniform of red or black t-shirts, their faces marked with clay in the manner of initiation candidates, and armed with traditional bows and arrows or *pangas* (machetes). The attacks by the Kalenjin warriors had in almost all cases been carried out by organized groups, and local Kalenjin often reported that outsiders had come to tell them that they had to fight and that the Kikuyu or others were planning to attack them. By contrast, where counter attacks had been mounted by Kikuyu, Luhya or Luo, they were usually more disorganized in character, and by no means as effective in driving people away from their land. The great majority of those displaced were members of the Kikuyu, Luo and Luhya ethnic groups.

Moreover, eyewitnesses consistently alleged that members of the security forces had failed to take any action against the attackers. In some cases, police who were present at the scene of an attack refused to respond to appeals for help, simply standing by and watching people being driven out of their houses. In others, police based at nearby posts would only arrive to assist clash victims well after attackers had left, despite earlier calls for action. Although attackers of all ethnic groups had been arrested, charges had been disproportionately pressed against members of the Kikuyu and other groups who in general had borne the brunt of the attacks. Often, individuals accused of serious offenses, including murder, had been released on bail despite continuing disturbances.[20] In September 1993, after two years of inaction in providing additional security, and soon after the highly publicized visits of representatives of two foreign human rights organizations to the clash areas, the government declared three "security operation zones" giving the police emergency-type powers, excluding "outsiders," and banning the carrying of weapons in the

---

[20] Human Rights Watch/Africa, *Divide and Rule*, pp.49-52. Kenya's criminal justice system has long been manipulated for political purposes. In 1988, judicial security of tenure was terminated, and a number of judges handing down decisions unfavorable to the government have been removed over the years.

worst-affected areas of Rift Valley Province.[21] The restrictions were lifted in March 1995. However, even when they were in place, the extra security precautions in these zones did not prevent an outbreak of violence in the Burnt Forest area in March 1994, which left at least eighteen dead and perhaps 25,000 displaced.[22] The attacks in Burnt Forest, which continued for a week despite government assurances of restored calm, left the disturbing impression that the government was unable or unwilling to take effective measures to stop the clashes.

Although the government has provided some assistance to clash victims, the vast majority of relief has been carried out by the church, either the NCCK or the Catholic church. The Kenyan Red Cross has also played a significant role. In October 1993, the United Nations Development Program (UNDP) and the Kenyan government announced a joint program for displaced people which proposed a $20 million plan for reconciliation and reintegration.[23] The program was intended to resettle the people displaced by the violence since 1991, estimated by UNDP at the time of the report at about 225,000. Appeals were made to the international community. However, many donors were slow to respond, privately citing reservations about the Kenyan government's commitment to ending the clashes. The program coincided with growing donor concerns about the violence. At the 1993 Consultative Group meeting to discuss renewal of Kenya's aid (which had been withheld pending political and economic liberalization), donors cited the ethnic violence as a concern.

While church and local relief organizations working with the displaced have welcomed the efforts begun by UNDP, they continue to have misgivings about the Kenyan government's commitment to the program. The success of the Kenyan government/UNDP proposal is ultimately contingent on the active involvement of the government to facilitate UNDP's efforts and to provide security. The Kenyan government has never undertaken a sustained program of action or sought a political solution to end the violence. Moreover, the government has

---

[21] The Preservation of Public Security (Molo, Burnt Forest and Londiani areas) regulations, 1993. Kenya Gazette supplement Number 60, September 17, 1993. Under the constitution, the president has the power to seal off any part of the country when public order is threatened. These powers are also set out in Part III of the Preservation of Public Security Act.

[22] Human Rights Watch/Africa, *Multipartyism Betrayed in Kenya*

[23] Government of Kenya/UNDP, *Program Document: Program for Displaced Persons*, Inter-agency joint programming (working document), October 26, 1993 .

actively obstructed genuine resettlement—with little protest from UNDP.

The Kenyan government has undermined UNDP, its implementing partner, on several occasions. However, UNDP has been extremely reluctant to criticize the Kenyan government, often going out of its way to term such incidents as "temporary hiccups" in the program. In January 1994, UNDP was denied access to Maela camp by armed policemen in what was later termed a "misunderstanding." One year later, when the government forcibly removed Maela camp residents and razed the camp to the ground, UNDP was not notified and was temporarily denied access to the camp.

It is difficult to assess how many people have returned to their land or been settled elsewhere through the resettlement program. However, an assertion by UNDP in 1994 that its program had resettled approximately one-third of the displaced created an uproar among local relief and church organizations.[24] Following these protests, the statement was recanted and UNDP accused the Kenyan press of manipulating the figure and quoting it out of context.[25] Local church organizations estimate that no more than 5 percent of the displaced have actually returned.

Reporting on events pertaining to the conflict has become increasingly difficult for journalists following negative international publicity of the government's role and inaction in ending violence. There have been numerous cases of government harassment of the press for reporting on the clashes including arrests without charge, the use of criminal charges such as subversion, police interrogation and the illegal impounding of issues which carry articles on the clashes. During the year and a half in which the Security Operations Regulations were in effect, the media was denied access to three of the worst-hit areas. According to the former Rift Valley provincial commissioner, Ishmael Chelang'a, the primary reason for the creation of the security zone was to keep away "those

---

[24] *From Relief to Rehabilitation, Reconstruction and Reconciliation*, draft report to the National Coordinating Committee for Displaced Persons by John Roggee, UNDO consultant, September 1994, p.2, subsection 4 and 5. In that report, UNDP stated "[f]or the whole of western Kenya, an optimistic estimate might be that one-third of the affected population is now back on its land and in the process of rebuilding its houses... A much larger proportion, perhaps as much as half of the total displaced in western Kenya, are in a transitional state of return.

[25] *"UNDP Official Disputes Resettlement Story," The Clashes Update*, The National Council of Churches of Kenya, Christian Outreach and Rural Development Services (Nairobi), Number 21, October 27, 1994, p. 1.

who did not wish us well and those who were spreading rumors, lies and propaganda."[26]

KANU politicians continue to call for the introduction of majimboism and the expulsion of all ethnic groups from the Rift Valley except for those pastoral groups—Kalenjins, Maasai, Turkana and Samburu—that were on land before colonialism. If implemented, the introduction of majimboism in this form would mean the resettlement of millions of members of other ethnic groups who have settled there since the 1920s and legally purchased land since the 1950s.

Others attempting to investigate allegations by clash victims or bring them together to discuss their problems have been charged with sedition or harassed in other ways.[27] By contrast, inflammatory statements by government ministers have gone uncensured. In November 1993, for example, Minister of Local Government and MP for Narok William ole Ntimama stated that he had "no regrets about the events in Enosuukia [where a group of Maasai had attacked and driven away thousands of Kikuyu living in a predominantly Maasai area] because the Maasai were fighting for their rights."[28] Ntimama was reported to have organized the Maasai attack on his own account: no measures were taken against him to investigate these charges or prevent him from repeating these and similar statements.

There has been a more general failure to investigate reports of the involvement or collusion of government officials in the violence, at all levels of responsibility. President Moi has consistently denied even the possibility that members of his government might be involved in instigating the clashes, alleging

---

[26] See Human Rights Watch/Africa, *Multipartism Betrayed*, p. 17.

[27] For example, Wangari Maathai, a well-known environmental activist, tried to organize a seminar for clash victims on three occasions in early 1993. On all three occasions, security police broke up the meeting. Koigi waWamwere, a former political prisoner and MP, faces charges of sedition because he was found to possess the publications of a group he co-founded in 1993, The National Democratic and Human Rights Organization (NDEHURIO) Later he was charged with armed robbery, in connection with a raid on a police station: he claims to have witnesses that he was hundreds of miles away at the time of the raid. Church workers carrying out relief have also been detained and harassed. Numerous sedition cases against journalists are outstanding. *Divide and Rule*, pp. 57-65; *Multipartyism Betrayed In Kenya*, pp 18-19 and 28-29.

[28] Minister: "No Regrets Over Events," *Daily Nation* (Nairobi), October 20, 1993.

instead that members of the opposition, journalists, church leaders and "certain foreign embassies" were stirring up tribal hatreds. Claiming from the outset that the clashes were the consequence of ethnic rivalries stirred up by multipartyism, he has repeated these claims to date despite all evidence to the contrary: in a speech in July 1994, Moi was reported to have"noted the imposition of Western type of democracy had precipitated bloodshed, hate and fragmentation in some African countries." [29]

Conclusion

Kenya is a multiethnic country, in which the tensions and conflicts introduced or exacerbated by colonial boundaries have continued to dominate post-independence politics. As in virtually all African countries, land is a crucial source of dispute between different ethnic groups. Yet no systematic effort has been made to address the shortage of arable land that faces a growing population. Instead, the government has manipulated these pressing problems to polarize ethnic sentiments to its political and economic advantage. The government has used the violence to reward and empower the Kalenjin and Maasai communities by allowing its members to occupy or buy land illegally in the Rift Valley Province, gaining its political allegiance and strengthening its economic base. Correspondingly, the violence has served to destabilize areas from which the political opposition would have been able to garner considerable support and to punish ethnic groups who have supported the political opposition.

The transformation of the Rift Valley Province into a Kalenjin landowning area also has significant political implications. Since that province is allocated the largest number of seats in Parliament (forty-four out of 188), the KANU government is making long-term political gains for a future election by consolidating Kalenjin political hegemony.

Although a long-term solution to the conflicts that have developed will eventually require greater equity in the distribution of land and other resources among ethnic groups, the evidence is clear that the immediate cause of Kenya's post-1991 "tribal clashes" has been the deliberate manipulation of existing tensions by government ministers, the differential application of the criminal justice system, and, above all, the organized provocation of violence by Kalenjin and Maasai members of the government anxious to prevent the installation of a government in which they would have lesser part. The solution to "tribal" violence is not less

---

[29] "President Moi says Western-Style democracy not a remedy for Africa," KNA News Agency, Nairobi, July 26, 1994 as reported in SWB AL/2059 A/5, July 28, 1994.

democracy but more.

FORMER YUGOSLAVIA

The wars that have raged in Croatia and Bosnia-Hercegovina since 1991 and 1992 respectively,[1] have been characterized by the "ethnic cleansing" of regions. In attempts to create "ethnically pure" areas, hundreds of thousands of individuals were killed and an additional two million forcibly displaced. The human rightes abuses associated with "ethnic cleansing"—summary executions, forced displacement, expulsion, internment in detention camps or ghettos, physical harassment and destruction of property—were systematically perpetrated by Serbian forces in Croatia and Bosnia.[2] Croatian forces in Bosnia and Croatia and the predominantly Muslim forces of the Bosnian government also have perpetrated similar abuses, albeit to varying degrees.[3]

Certain journalists, United Nations officials, and European and U.S. government policy-makers have portrayed the armed conflicts in Croatia and Bosnia as a civil war caused by a history of hatred between Serbs, Croats, and

---

[1] Hereinafter referred to as Bosnia.

[2] See the following reports by Human Rights Watch/Helsinki which document Serbian abuses in Croatia and Bosnia: *Yugoslavia: Human Rights Abuses in the Craotian Conflict*, September 1991; Letter to Slobodan Milosevic, President of the Republic of Serbia, and General Blagoje Adzic, then Minister of Defense and Chief of Staff of the Yugoslav People's Army, January 21, 1992; *War Crimes in Bosnia-Hercegovina, Volume I*, August 1992; *War Crimes in Bosnia-Hercegovina, Volume II*, April 1993; *Abuses Continue in the Former Yugoslavia: Serbia, Montenegro and Bosnia-Hercegovina*, July 1993; *Prosecute Now! Helsinki Watch Releases Eight Cases for War Crimes Tribunal on Former Yugoslavia*, August 1, 1993; *The War Crimes Tribunal: One Year Later*, February 1994; *War Crimes in Bosnia-Hercegovina: Bosanski Šamac*, April 1994; and *War Crimes in Bosnia-Hercegovina: UN Cease-Fire Won't Help Banja Luka*, June 1994.

[3] See the following reports by Human Rights Watch/Helsinki which document abuses by Croatian forces in Croatia proper, by the Bosnian Croat militia, by Muslim paramilitary groups and by the predominantly Muslim forces of the Bosnian government: *Yugoslavia: Human Rights Abuses in the Croatian Conflict*, September 1991; Letter to Franjo Tudjman, President of the Republic of Croatia, February 13, 1992; *Prosecute Now! Helsinki Watch Releases Eight Cases for War Crimes Tribunal on Former Yugoslavia*, August 1, 1993; *Bosnia-Hercegovina: Abuses by Bosnian Croat and Muslim Forces in Central and Southwestern Bosnia-Hercegovina*, September 1993; and *The War Crimes Tribunal: One Year Later*, February 1994.

Muslims. Indeed, some individuals or communities in the former Yugoslavia[4] harbor resentment toward other ethnic groups whom they view as responsible for past repression. But resentment between various nationalities is not the primary cause of the bloodbath that is now underway in the Balkans. Rather, communal violence was orchestrated by certain politicians, bureaucrats, and members of the army as a means through which to retain political power and forcibly acquire territory.

Background
    In the former Yugoslavia, a distinction was drawn between the terms "nationality" or "nation," on the one hand, and "ethnicity," on the other. The former Yugoslavia was a state composed of six republics, in which one nationality was predominant; i.e., Croats were the majority in Croatia, Slovenes in Slovenia, Muslims in Bosnia, Serbs in Serbia, Montenegrins in Montenegro and

---

    [4] Prior to the outbreak of war, the population of the former Yugoslavia was approximately 23 million. The demographic information for each of the republics that comprised the former Yugoslavia is taken from the 1991 census and is as follows:
- Serbia (including the province of Vojvodina and Kosovo): total population = 9.7 million, of which 65.8 percent are Serbs, 17.2 percent Albanian, 3.5 percent Hungarian and 13.5 percent which identified itself as "Yugoslav" or a member of another nationality.
- Montenegro: total population = 615,000, of which 61.8 percent were Montenegrins, 14.6 percent Muslims, 6.6 percent Albanians, 17 percent which identified itself as "Yugoslav" or a member of another nationality.
- Macedonia: total population = 2 million, of which 64.6 percent are Macedonians and 21.8 percent are Albanians, 16.6 percent which identified itself as "Yugoslav" or a member of another nationality.
- Bosnia-Hercegovina: total population = 4.3 million, of which 43.7 percent were Muslims, 31.4 percent Serbs, 17.3 Croats, and 7.6 percent which identified itself as "Yugoslav" or a member of another nationality.
- Croatia: total population = 4.7 million, of which 77.9 percent were Croats, 12.2 percent Serbs and 9.9 percent which identified itself as "Yugoslav" or a member of another nationality.
- Slovenia: total population = 1.9 million, of which 87.5 percent are Slovenes, and 12.5 percent which identified itself as "Yugoslav" or a member of another nationality.
(Albanians in the republic of Macedonia and the province of Kosovo boycotted the 1991 census as a form of protest against the Macedonian and Serbian governments, which they did not trust to adequately report the real number of the Albanians in each respective area.)

Macedonians in Macedonia. "Ethnic minorities" were those nationalities that were not "constituent nations" of the former Yugoslavia but whose "mother country" lay elsewhere, i.e. Hungarians, Albanians, Italians, and Slovaks. Claiming to be a "constituent nation" of the former Yugoslavia, some Serbs justified Serbian claims to land in Croatia and Bosnia. Similar justification was used by some Croats to justify Croatian claims to land in Bosnia. However, the Serbian government has denied similar territorial and political claims to Albanians in Kosovo, claiming that, as a "minority" they did not have the same rights to territory as the "constituent nations" of the former Yugoslavia and the territorial claims by Albanians must be sought within Albania where they are a "constituent nation."

In 1986, Slobodan Milošević assumed control of Serbia's communist party and became the de facto ruler of the Serbia. During the same year, the Serbian Academy of Arts and Sciences issued a "Memorandum" which portrayed Serbs as disenfanchised in Yugoslavia and called for the reassertion of Serbian interests in the country. Recognizing the waning appeal of communist ideology in Yugoslavia, Milošević substituted nationalism for communism as a mechanism through which to maintain and consolidate political power. By the late 1980s, Milošević succeeded in assuming de facto control over the communist parties of Kosovo, Vojvodina, and Montenegro in addition to Serbia proper. Having consolidated power in the eastern part of the country, Milošević advocated the maintenance of a strong centralized regime based in Belgrade, the capital of Serbia and the base of his power.

During the same period, segments of Slovenian society, including the press and some members of the Slovenian government, began a campaign aimed at reassertion of Slovenian interests. Much of their effort was directed towards the promotion of economic and political reforms that would benefit Slovenia rather than the federal Belgrade-based government. In contrast to the Serbian government's view of a strong centralized state, the reform-oriented Slovenian government called for the reconstitution of Yugoslavia as a decentralized confederation which would allow each of the country's republics greater political and economic freedom.

In 1988, three journalists who worked for the liberal Slovenian magazine *Mladina* were accused by the federal government and army of "disclosing state military secrets" and were sentenced to several years in prison in a political trial. The *Mladina* case increased tensions between the Slovenian public and the Belgrade authorities—particularly the Yugoslav People's Army (Jugoslavenska Narodna Armija (JNA))—on the other hand. In contrast to the Serbian government's view of a strong centralized state, the more liberal Slovenian communist party called for the reconstitution of Yugoslavia as a decentralized confederation which would allow each of the country's republics greater political and economic freedom.

In 1987, the Serbian government under Milošević began a policy of repression in Kosovo. Autonomy granted to Kosovo in 1974 was revoked and the provincial government was put under the direct control of the Belgrade authorities which used mistreatment in detention, arbitrary arrests of Albanians, restrictions on press freedom and other violations of civil and political rights to enforce its rule in the region. During the mid-1980s and especially the late 1980s, public sentiment against Milošević's politics and his repression in Kosovo increased in Slovenia, Croatia, Macedonia and Bosnia. The contentious positions of the Serbian and Slovenian communist parties led to a walk-out of the Slovene delegation at a meeting of the communist parties of Yugoslavia. The Croatian delegation soon followed suit.

In multi-party elections in each of the republics in 1990, Milošević was elected president of Serbia, which allowed him to maintain power throughout Serbia (including Vojvodina and Kosovo) while his supporters retained power in Montenegro. Liberal communists retained power in Slovenia and Macedonia while Croatia and Bosnia elected primarily non-communist, nationalist, candidates to their parliaments and as presidents of their respective republics.[5]

Following the 1990 elections, the presidents of the six republics held a series of meetings to determine the future make-up of Yugoslavia. While Serbia and Montenegro continued to lobby for the maintenance of centralized state, Slovenia and Croatia called for a confederation. Macedonia and Bosnia were willing to compromise between the two positions but tended to sympathize with the views espoused by Croatia and Slovenia.

During this time, Yugoslavia was headed by a collective presidency composed of representatives from each of the republics. The representatives to the presidency rotated control of the body for one-year periods. Although Vojvodina and Kosovo were provinces within Serbia, each also had a representative. Serbian control over Vojvodina and Kosovo and Montenegro's alliance with Serbia resulted in Serbia's de facto control of four votes on the eight-member presidency. In mid-1991, when the Croatian representative was due to assume control of the presidency, the representatives of Serbia, Montenegro, Vojvodina and Kosovo

---

[5] Franjo Tudjman, the president-elect of Croatia, had been a general of the Yugoslav People's Army (Jugoslavenska Narodna Armija - JNA), which was strongly communist in orientation. Tudjman had fallen out of favor with the communists in the 1970s and had been a political prisoner in the early 1980s. His platform for election as Croatia's president was highly nationalistic and anti-communist.

blocked his appointment and tensions between the various republics increased. The collective presidency dissolved shortly thereafter.

Throughout this period, Serbian nationalism continued to grow and the Serbian press began to depict Serbs as persecuted in Kosovo, Croatia and Bosnia, areas where they were not the majority ethnic group. Such disinformation was channelled not only within Serbia proper but also to Kosovo and Serbian-populated areas of Croatia and Bosnia. In reaction to Milošević's propaganda and in a bid to stay in power, Slovenian, Muslim and especially Croatian politicians began to develop their own propaganda, which portrayed their respective nationalities as the victims of Serbian hegemony.

Tensions between the republics increased to such an extent that four of the six republics of the former Yugoslavia seceded from the country: Slovenia and Croatia seceded in June 1991, Macedonia in January 1991, and Bosnia-Hercegovina in April 1992. Following Slovenia's secession from Yugoslavia, JNA troops were sent to the republic to prevent it from assuming control of its international borders. After several days of fighting, the JNA withdrew from the republic due to Slovenian armed resistance and also for lack of indigenous support in an area which did not have a Serbian minority.

Milošević and the JNA then turned to Croatia, seeking to assume control over that republic by manipulating the Serbs who comprised 12.5 percent of Croatia's population. In August 1990 rebel Serbs in Croatia, supported by the Serbian government, rebelled against the Croatian government and assumed parts of Croatia.

The Arming and Training of Serbian Troops in Croatia and Bosnia by the Government of Serbia Proper and the Yugoslav Army (JNA)

The Serbian government, under the leadership of Milošević armed extremist Serbs in parts of Croatia and Bosnia. Members of paramilitary groups armed and trained by the Serbian regime later perpetrated the most vicious human rights violations against non-Serbs in Croatia and Bosnia. Also, JNA troops and paramilitary forces from Serbia proper provided logistical or other support to, and in some cases participated in battle with, indigenous Serbian forces. These JNA and paramilitary troops are also responsible for egregious human rights abuses in Croatia and Bosnia.

The Serbian Interior Ministry has long been and still is the stronghold of Milošević's power. This ministry—with assistance by the predominantly Serbian officer corps of the JNA[6]—armed and trained extremist Serbs in areas of Croatia and Bosnia where Serbs consituted a majority or significant minority prior to the secession of Croatia and Bosnia from the former Yugoslavia, in 1991 and 1992 respectively.[7] Many of the rebel Serbs who were armed and trained by the JNA, Serbian Interior Ministry, and paramilitary forces from Serbia proper, were extremist members of the Serbian Democratic Party (Srpska Demokratska Stanka (SDS)), the political party whose branches in Croatia and Bosnia represented portions of the Serbian population in each republic.

Serbian paramilitary groups based in Serbia proper also were armed and trained—primarily by the Serbian Interior Ministry which was then headed by Mihajlo Kertes—for the purposes of fighting a rebellion in Croatia and Bosnia.[8] Leaders of some paramilitary forces from Serbia proper have since been accused of war crimes and crimes against humanity by the U.S. government, Human Rights Watch/Helsinki and others including Željko Ražnjatović (a.k.a. Arkan), leader of the paramilitary force known as the "Tigers;" Vojislav Šešelj, President of the Serbian Radical Party and the Serbian Četnik Movement;[9] and Dragoslav Bokan and Mirko Jović, both leaders of paramilitary forces originally based in Serbia proper.

By August 1990 in Croatia, rebel Serbs assumed power in the town of Knin and continued to take over territory throughout the Krajina region and eastern Slavonia until a full-scale war broke out between Croatian government forces and rebel Serb units in early July 1991. By the time a tenuous peace pact was signed in January 1992, Serbs had occupied approximately 30 percent of Croatia's territory and had assumed control over large parts of Bosnia, eventually assuming control of approximately 70 percent of that republic by late 1992.

---

[6] Although the JNA recruits reflected the ethnic composition of the former Yugoslavia, the JNA officer corps was predominantly Serbian.

[7] Evidence of efforts by Milošević and the JNA to arm and train rebel Serbs in Croatia and Bosnia is contained in the memoirs Veljko Kadijević, the head of the JNA at the time of the Serbian rebellion in Croatia in 1990. (See Veljko Kadijević, *Moje Vidjenje Raspada* (Belgrade: Politika, 1993).)

[8] Ibid.

[9] Šešelj and members of his Serbian Radical Party have since fallen out of favor with the Milošević regime but his paramilitary forces—and those trained by his troops—continue to operate in Serbian-controlled areas of Croatia and Bosnia.

The Serbian government and the JNA defended their earliest assault on Slovenia in late June 1991 and their support for rebel Serbs in Croatia and Bosnia citing three reasons, all of which are faulty. First, the Serbian government and the JNA defended the use of armed force in Slovenia, Croatia and Bosnia claiming the three republics had unilaterally seceded without taking the interests of the Serbs into account. This argument ignores the fact that the presidents of the various republics had met for months to discuss the future make-up of the former Yugoslavia and that it was the intrasigence of Milošević's delegation that had prevented a compromise. Also, few Serbs lived in Slovenia, prior to that republic's secession.[10] Despite the Croatian government's nationalist character, it did offer a degree of autonomy to Serbs in the Krajina region prior to the outbreak of war in the 1991 and provided for Serbian representation in parliament. Rebel Serbs rejected what they viewed as the insufficient degree of autonomy offered by the Croatian government, which they viewed as the reincarnation of the Croatian Nazi puppet state during World War II. Rebel Serbs also walked out of the Croatian parliament, citing hostility toward them by members of the ruling party. Despite the shortcomings of these offers by the Croatian government, rebel Serbs in Croatia preferred to take up arms rather than negotiate a settlement with the Croatian government. Similarly in Bosnia, extremist Serbs chose not to work within the Bosnian legislature, which had been fractionalized along ethnic lines but in which inter-ethnic discussion was on-going. In sum, when the former Yugoslavia was still one state, rebel Serbs had already armed themselves and chose to fight for their interests through the use of force, not within the framework of their respective republican government's structure.

Secondly, the Serbian government argued that the use of force in Croatia and Bosnia was used to protect the Serbs living in those two republics from persecution by the "fascist" Croatian regime and the "fundamentalist" Bosnian government. Human Rights Watch/Helsinki representatives travelled to Croatia (in August, October, and November 1990 and in March 1991) and Bosnia (in June 1991) to investigate the status of the various nationalities—particularly the Serbs—in both republics. During the missions to Croatia, it was clear that the Croatian government of Franjo Tudjman was nationalistic and highly insensitive to Serbian concerns. However, it did not systematically seek to cleanse all Serbs from Croatia. Thirdly, there is absolutely no evidence to support the claim that Serbs were persecuted as a group in Bosnia prior to the outbreak of war in that republic.

Lastly, the Serbian government and the JNA justified the use of force in

---

[10] According to the 1991 census, cite population figures for Slovenia.

Slovenia, Croatia and Bosnia claiming they had a right and a responsibility to maintain the territorial integrity of the former Yugoslavia. However, if rebel Serbs, the Serbian government and the JNA sought to maintain the former Yugoslavia as a multi-ethnic state of six republics, the systematic expulsion, murder and internment of non-Serbs would not have been necessary. Rather, the use of "ethnic cleansing" by Serbian and JNA forces supports the creation of a "Greater Serbia," not the preservation of a multi-ethnic Yugoslavia.

In addition to arming and training rebel Serbs in Croatia and Bosnia, JNA and paramilitary forces from Serbia proper coordinated and participated in military operations and perpetrated human rights abuses alongside indigenous Serbian forces in the two republics. When fighting first broke out between Croats and rebel Serbs in Croatia, the JNA positioned itself between the two groups, thereby allowing Serbian forces to consolidate control over their territorial gains. When the JNA did intervene, it was at times when Serbian forces appeared to be losing; similar support was not given to Croatian forces. Moreover, rebel Serb forces were allowed to sieze weapons belonging to the JNA and the territorial defense units[11] while Croatian and Bosnian government forces were prevented from doing the same. Later, JNA troops fought openly on behalf of Serbian troops in Croatia and Bosnia.

In almost all cases in which fighting took place, a pattern involving JNA troops or forces from Serbia proper emerged. In many large-scale field operations

---

[11] After World War II and during Tito's reign, the official Yugoslav position maintained that Yugoslavia, as a non-aligned state, was surrounded by external enemies, such as the North Atlantic Treaty Organization (NATO) to the west and the Warsaw Pact to the east. In light of these "threats," Yugoslavia had to be prepared to defend its "territorial integrity, unity and independence." In preparation for possible attacks from "outside enemies," weapons for the general population were stored at the local level throughout the country. The weapons were purchased from workers' revenues at local enterprises and kept in various storage areas throughout each locality. Each of Yugoslavia's six constituent republics maintained a territorial defense (teritorijalna o(d)brana - TO) structure, which included a civilian security force (civilna zaštita) and a local reserve militia. All former soldiers who served in the federal army could be called up to serve as reserve police officers for the republican police force or members of the local territorial defense unit. The TO's weapons could be distributed by the republican government, in consultation with the federal army and the federal government. Most of the weapons stored in territorial defense arsenals in Croatia were confiscated by the Yugoslav Army (JNA) prior to the outbreak of war in that republic. The TO arsenals in Serbian-controlled areas of Bosnia-Hercegovina also have been confiscated by Serbian paramilitaries and the JNA.

in Croatia and Bosnia, heavy weaponry, grid coordinates and other logistical support was provided to the rebel Serb forces by the JNA. The siege of a village, town or city was then conducted with those weapons, either by indigenous Serbs or in conjunction with JNA and paramilitary forces from Serbia proper. When the area was about to fall or had surrendered, Serbian paramilitary forces entered the area to conduct "cleansing" operations aimed at killing or detaining remaining civilians and combatants. Most men between the ages of eighteen and fifty-five were summarily executed or taken to prisons and detention camps where they were brutally tortured. Women, children and elderly persons also were interned and many were mistreated and often women were raped. JNA troops facilitated, participated in or stood by as Serbian paramilitaries trained and armed by the JNA "cleansed" an area of non-Serbs.

In addition to the use of JNA-owned war material, Serbian forces also used JNA-operated prisons and detention centers (such as Stara Gradiška in northern Bosnia and Sremska Mitrovica in the Vojvodina region of Serbia) to detain and torture captured combatants and civilians. JNA personnel were directly responsible for the administration of most such prisons and the abuses perpetrated therein. The fall of the city of Vukovar in Croatia in November 1991 is one example of military and other coordination between forces belonging to indigenous rebel Serbs, paramilitary forces from Serbia proper and the JNA. The JNA bears equal responsibility with Serbian paramilitary forces for the siege of Vukovar and the abuses perpetrated after the fall of the city and during the internment of the city's survivors, most of whom were detained in the republic of Serbia. The perpetration of human rights abuses and other involvement of the JNA and paramilitary groups from Serbia proper also was particularly evident in most of eastern Bosnia in April and May 1992, when most of the non-Serbs were expelled from the area or killed.

The active involvement of the Serbian government and the JNA—an allegedly neutral entity committed to protecting all the peoples of the former Yugoslavia—on behalf of rebel Serbian forces points to the fact that the violence in Croatia and Bosnia was planned and carefully orchestrated and facilitated by government agencies and actors.

Government Manipulation of the Mass Media

The Serbian, Croatian and Bosnian governments have all manipulated the state-owned media to foment ethnic hatred. As stated above, Milošević initiated a propaganda campaign aimed at portraying the Serbs as victims in the former Yugoslavia as early as 1987 in order to gain public support for his campaign in Kosovo. At the height of the war in Croatia in 1991, Serbian television showed frequent films about the atrocities perpetrated against Serbs by the Nazi-aligned Croatian Ustaša. Similar films portraying the fate of the Serbs under Ottoman rule also were shown. Such programs were broadcast at times when tensions between Serbs, Albanians, Croats and Muslims were at their highest. The Serbian media in Bosnia (SRNA) and Croatia all propagated the positions held by the Serbian government and, in most cases, perpetuated hatred of the ethnic group(s) which they were fighting directly.

In addition to state sponsorship of propaganda and misinformation, Serbian authorities also censored the press and imposed a partial information blockade in areas under their control. Portions of the Serbian opposition which had been against the war were not given adequate time in the state-owned media to express their opinions. Indepedent radio stations were prevented from broadcasting outside the greater Belgrade area. In most regions outside of Belgarde, state-sponsored Radio and Television Serbia is the only news to which the public has access via the electronic media. Several purges of journalists working in the state-owned press ensured that the Serbian media complied with the position espoused by Milošević's regime. In addition to official propaganda, Serbian authorities in Croatia and Bosnia jammed, at various times, Croatian and Bosnian television and radio programs and have prevented non-Serbian papers from entering Serbian-held areas.

To substantiate claims of impending "genocide," Serbian state media manipulated facts. For example, after the city of Vukovar fell to Serbian forces in November 1991, Television Belgrade[12] showed pictures of the dead who had been killed during the fighting, usually due to shrapnel or gunfire wounds. Because of the ferocity of the Serbs' siege of the city, the Vukovar hospital staff could not bury their bodies and lined the corpses outside the hospital. When Serbian forces took the city, Television Belgrade claimed that all of the dead were Serbs and that some had been "massacred" by the Croats. The bodies later were taken to a military hospital in Belgrade, where autopsies were performed and an attempt to identify the victims was made. Human Rights Watch/Helsinki representatives spoke to a doctor involved in this work, and he claimed that these dead were not all Serbs[13] and that the victims had died as a result of shrapnel and gunfire wounds inflicted

---

[12] Television Belgrade has since been renamed Television Serbia.

[13] Prior to the siege, the municipality of Vukovar had a population of 84,024, of which 43.7 percent were Croats, 37.4 percent were Serbs, and 7.3 percent identified themselves as "Yugoslavs." Hungarians, Slovaks, Ruthenes, Germans and others comprised the remaining 11.6 percent of Vukovar's inhabitants.

during the siege. According to the doctor, the bodies he examined—which numbered in the hundreds—had not been summarily executed or massacred. Despite these facts, the footage and narration of "massacred Serbs in Vukovar" was broadcast on Serbian television for days.

Similarly, the Croatian and Bosnian governments followed suit with their breed of propaganda. During the fighting between Muslims and Croats in southwestern and central Bosnia—primarily in mid-1993—the Croatian government reported and, in some cases exaggerated, abuses perpetrated by the predominantly Muslim forces of the Bosnian Army but excluded similar or worse abuses committed by the Bosnian Croat militia (HVO). For example, Croatian television downplayed HVO's siege of Mostar and the systematic expulsion and detention of Muslims in Hercegovina during the spring and summer of 1993, while sensationalizing the flight of Croats from central Bosnia. Also, as early as October 1992, Croatian television misrepresented attacks by the HVO in Prozor as assaults by Muslim "fundamentalists" against Croatian civilians when, in fact, the opposite was true.

Although the Bosnian government continues to support a multi-ethnic country, the state-owned television also has exacerbated ethnic tensions at times. The incitement of ethnic hatred in the Bosnian press was pronounced during fighting between Muslims and Croats in central Bosnia. The Bosnian government-controlled television downplayed or failed to report abuses prepetrated by its troops against Serbs and Croats. Certain members of the Bosnian government used inflammatory language against Croats and Serbs during the battles between Bosnian Army forces and the respective Serb and Croat militias in Bosnia. Abuses perpetrated by Bosnian Army soldiers in Tarčin, Konjic and elsewhere were rarely, if ever, reported.

Impunity

Human rights abuses related to the wars in Bosnia and Croatia are committed on a massive scale, yet, few persons have been held accountable for their crimes. The fact that human rights abuses are perpetrated on such a wide scale and the lack of punishment for such abuses indicates that that the violence is not only orchestrated by state actors, but is condoned by them as well.

As stated above, most "cleansing" operations followed battles or sieges in mid- and late 1991 in Croatia and in mid- and late 1992 in Bosnia. During these times, the JNA was actively involved in the fighting in both republics and cannot claim ignorance of abuses. Moreover, when the JNA nominally pulled out of Bosnia on May 19, 1992, it left its weaponry and ammunition to Bosnian Serb forces which perpetrated many of the human rights abuses against non-Serbs with the aid of, or in conjunction with, the JNA during the early months of the war. Serbian forces responsible for abuses during the siege and after the fall of Vukovar were based in, and supplied from, Serbia proper. The prisoners incarcerated after the fall of Vukovar were held in Serbia proper, particularly in JNA-operated prison in Sremska Mitrovica and elsewhere in Serbia. Other detention facilities such as Begejći and Stajičevo—in the Vojvodina province of Serbia—also were used to incarcerate and torture predominantly Croatian prisoners of war and civilians after the fall of Vukovar. The JNA-operated prison in Stara Gradiška in Serbian-controlled areas of Croatia, was used to incarcerate and mistreat non-Serbs from Croatia and Bosnia. The use of JNA-operated prisons and other detention facilities in Serbia proper indicate that the JNA leadership and Serbian government were aware of, and condoned, the establishment of such facilities and are therefore ultimately responsible for abuses perpetrated therein.

The abuses committed by Serbian forces in Croatia and Bosnia were perpetrated on such a wide scale and in such a systematic fashion, that high-level and local Bosnian Serb authorities and military commanders could not have remained ignorant of their commission by troops under their control. The fact that these abuses continued—indeed increased—over time and that virtually no one was punished for such crimes, indicates at least the tolerance and acceptance of such abuses by the Bosnian Sreb authorities. Similar impunity for the systematic and well-organized abuses by the HVO against Muslims in the Mostar and Čapljina municipalities implicate the Bosnian Croat military and civilian authorities and the Croatian government, as their sponsor.

Moreover, JNA officers responsible for the siege of certain cities and attacks on civilian targets in Bosnia and Croatia have been promoted, rather than expelled from, the JNA. For example, Major Šljivančanin, the JNA officer responsible for the siege of Vukovar and abuses perpetrated thereafter, was promoted within the JNA officer corps. Major Momčilo Perišić, the JNA officer responsible for the attacks on the cities of Zadar in Croatia and Mostar in Bosnia[14] was promoted as head of the JNA in August 1993. Ratko Mladić, the man responsible for Serbian forces in the Knin and Krajina region of Croatia, later was made commander of Bosnian Serb forces, in which capacity he has been responsible for countless attacks against civilians. In most cases, those responsible

---

[14] During the early stages of the war in Bosnia, Serbian forces were the first to attack the city of Mostar, which was then defended jointly by Croats and Muslims. However, by May 1993, Croatian and Muslim forces began fighting each other and the Bosnian Croat militia (HVO) has been responsible for much of the destruction and civilian loss of life in the city since then.

for the most brutal abuses have been rewarded, rather than punished, by Serbian authorities. Such action does not indicate a willingness to prevent or stop—nor to hold accountable those responsible for—human rights abuses, the vast majority of which have been perpetrated along ethnic lines.

The military conquests of Serbian forces in Croatia and Bosnia and the impunity with which they conducted their brutal "ethnic cleansing" campaigns in pursuit of their territorial goals, prompted Croat and Muslim forces to follow suit and commit similar abuses in the hope of improving their success on the battlefield. Hundreds of thousands of Muslims who had been forcibly displaced by Serbian forces fled to areas in which Croats and Muslims were allied. Demographic shifts, lack of appropriate housing and rising political tensions in areas held jointly by Muslims and Croats contributed to the eventual outbreak of war between the two groups. Ethnic fighting in Bosnia has become intra-ethnic. In the areas north of Bihać, Muslim forces loyal to the Sarajevo-based Bosnian government—which opposes concessions to Serbian forces—continue to fight dissident Muslim forces loyal to businessman Fikret Abdić, which argue for negotiation and accomodation with the Serbs. Despite the formation of a Muslim-Croat alliance and Bosnia re-gaining control over Bihac, tensions between the respective groups continue.

Conclusion: The Legitimation of "Ethnic Cleansing"

Representatives from the United Nations, the European Union and the so-called "contact group" (i.e., US, Russia, Germany France and Britain) have based their hopes for peace in Croatia and particularly in Bosnia primarily on the division of territory. The fact that such territory was acquired through the use of "ethnic cleansing" and military attacks against civilians has largely been tolerated by international negotiators. Little effort has been made to facilitate the repatriation of the displaced, to protect civilians living in areas dominated by forces of another ethnic group, or to bring to justice those responsible for war crimes and crimes against humanity in Croatia and Bosnia. The continued omission of these provisions from any peace plan will legitimize "ethnic cleansing" and undermine prospects for a lasting peace in the former Yugoslavia. It also will encourage other abusive regimes to foment inter-ethnic hatred as a means through which to achieve their political or military goals.

LEBANON

The Lebanese civil war, which lasted from 1975 to 1990 and claimed the lives of nearly 200,000 people, has been frequently portrayed as a communal conflict caused by religious hatred. While acknowledging that Lebanese parties have carried out most of the horrendous slaughter and destruction, many Lebanese, object to the religious characterization and the use of the terms civil war or communal warfare, claiming that the conflict was imposed on Lebanon by outside powers. They blame Arab states, Israel, the Palestinians, Iran, the Soviet Union and the United States for the civil war, claiming that these competing powers exploited Lebanon's diversity and used the country, because of its weak government and feeble army, merely as a battleground to settle their accounts. Both opposing characterizations contain some truth. While much of the violence exploded along religious lines with elements of social and economic disparity, there was also ample evidence that outside powers played an active role in instigating and fueling communal violence. Regional political dynamics, primarily the Israeli-Palestinian conflict, contributed to Lebanon's communal warfare. But perhaps the most significant factor behind Lebanon's communal violence is the sectarian-based "confessional" state structure and internal political maneuvering and exploitation of sectarian differences to maintain it. Government positions, power, and privileges were apportioned to recognized religiously-defined communities through secular leaders. To preserve these privileges, the leaders used various means—including incitement of sectarian violence, control of information, human rights restrictions, and inviting outside intervention—to maintain the system that sanctioned them.

Background

In the early nineteenth century, Ottoman officials sought to increase their influence over Mount Lebanon by fomenting family rivalries and exacerbating religious differences. These attempts to divide and rule were initially unsuccessful. However, in 1858, the Ottoman Empire's adoption of the Land Code, permitting private land ownership, led to a major economic and social upheaval; Maronite peasants rose up against landlords. Fearing a revolt from the Maronite peasantry on Druze plantations, Druze feudal lords launched a preemptive strike, with Turkish officials' complicity, and massacred Maronite villagers. In 1860, France and other European powers intervened, ostensibly to protect the Christians. One year later foreign powers imposed the Réglament Organique, by which the Ottoman government designated Mount Lebanon as an autonomous Ottoman province to be ruled by a non-Lebanese Ottoman Christian governor selected by the sultan and approved by the great powers. In 1864, under the authority of the

Réglament, a twelve-member council was established to assist the governor. Seats in the new council were allocated on a sectarian basis: four for the Maronites, three for the Druze, two for the Greek Orthodox and one each for Greek Catholics, Shi`a Muslims and Sunni Muslims. The new system, which continued until the end of Ottoman rule in 1918, weakened the feudal structure, but replaced it with a closed sectarian system that steadily increased Maronite power at the expense of the Druze and other sects.[1] Following its defeat in World War One, Turkey lost Lebanon and Syria to France which secured a League of Nations mandate to rule the two territories.

In 1920, France established Greater Lebanon by annexing Beirut, Tripoli, Sidon and Tyre to Mount Lebanon. The inclusion of new territory bringing communities of Sunni and Shi`a Muslims to the original Maronite and Druze of Mount Lebanon dramatically altered the demographic makeup. Instead of setting up a secular government, the French colonial authorities opted for a sectarian-based system in which the president would always be a Maronite, and the lesser position of prime minister would always be occupied by a Muslim. Based on a 1933 census which showed a slight Christian majority, it was decided that legislative seats would be divided in a ratio of 11:9 in favor of Christians.[2] Throughout the 1940s, Christians as well as Muslims became increasingly disenchanted with French rule and demanded independence. In November 1943, the French authorities responded by arresting the president, a Maronite Christian, and suspending the constitution. But demands for independence persisted and unrest increased. Under pressure from independent Arab states, Britain and the U.S., France eventually relinquished its rule of Lebanon, with the condition that the sectarian-based government system remain in place.

---

[1] "The fate of Lebanon was sealed," according to a Lebanese sociologist, "for from that moment on, all political representation and all political activities until this very day will be intimately connected with religious affiliation." Safia Antoun Saadeh, *The Social Structure of Lebanon: Democracy or Servitude?* (Editions Dar an-Nahar, Beirut, 1993), p. 53.

[2] Muslim leaders in Lebanon have frequently disputed the accuracy of this census. To avoid an extremely sensitive issue, no other census has been conducted since, but it is now generally acknowledged that Muslims constitute a majority and that the Shi`a, not the Sunnis, are the largest Muslim community. However, Christians point out that most Lebanese who have over the years emigrated but maintained their Lebanese citizenship are Christian. According to most accounts Christians would be a clear majority if emigrants were included.

Post-Independence Power Struggle

The confessional system (later known as the National Pact) set up by the French continued to form the basis of the Lebanese state. Although the community units were defined in religious terms, the political leaders were influential heads of prominent families, not clerics. Selected by Parliament, they presumed the role of interlocutors for their respective sects, garnering influence for themselves and doling out government largesse to their supporters. Leaders of the Maronite and Sunni sects in particular bolstered their positions at the top of the sectarian pyramid and frequently spoke on behalf of all Christians and all Muslims, respectively.[3] The system became even more sectarian in 1952 when a new election law increased the electoral districts from five to thirty-three, (forty-four seats). The new districts were drawn according to sectarian affiliation, as estimated in the disputed 1933 census. Of forty-four seats, twenty-four (55 percent) were allotted to Christians (thirteen Maronites, eleven other sects) and twenty (forty-five percent) to Muslims (nine Sunnis, eight Shi`a and three Druze). Four years later, an amendment to the electoral law increased the number of seats to sixty-six, without affecting the proportions.

In 1952, Camille Sham`oun, a Maronite was selected by the parliament to be president. Alarmed by the growing pan-Arab influence of President Nasser of Egypt, the pro-Western Sham'oun sought to amend the constitution to enable him to run for a second six-year term. Facing stiff opposition from Nasser's supporters in Lebanon, Sham`oun tried to rally the support of other Maronite leaders, but was only partially successful. He then sought assistance from the U.S., which was already providing significant aid under the Eisenhower Doctrine. The fundamentally different views of national identity—Lebanon's Arab and Western—surfaced in the opposition to Sham`oun's pro-U.S. policies, especially among Muslims and Orthodox Christians who favored the Arab nationalist movement led by Nasser.

Popular unrest and anti-Western demonstrations spread during 1957. The government's draconian response of arbitrarily arresting several hundred activists, including over one hundred Lebanese Communists, made matters worse. After a spate of bombings and assassinations shook Lebanon in late 1957, Sham`oun purged from the cabinet most opponents of his pro-Western positions. Then, in an attempt to obscure the anti-Western sentiment of the opposition, the government mounted a media campaign (a tactic that would be repeated in later years) which misrepresented the differences as a conflict between Christians (pro-Lebanese sovereignty) and Muslims (pro-Arab unity). Although the Maronite patriarch,

---

[3] Safia Antoun Saadeh, *The Social Structure of Lebanon.*

among other Christian leaders, rejected this characterization and opposed the
president, the government propaganda succeeded in convincing many Christians.
President Sham oun boldly called for additional security aid from the U.S., to
which the Eisenhower administration quickly responded. The U.S. Sixth Fleet
arrived in July with 10,000 U.S. Marines, who landed in Beirut to shore up the
government's forces. In the meantime, Maronite-led government troops and
Maronite militias battled an alliance of Muslim militias and their leftist and
Nasserist allies in Tripoli, Beirut, Sidon and Tyre. The crisis was defused in the
fall of 1958 when President Sham'oun dropped his plans for a second term, U.S.
troops withdrew and Parliament chose as president, Fou'ad Shihab, a Maronite
general with broad support among Muslims and Christians.

By the end of the 1957-58 events, most Lebanese concluded that what the
government media described as communal strife was largely a struggle resulting
from Sham'oun's presidential ambition and his rivals' determination to deprive him
of a second term. And in the process, the broader clash between Arab and Western
orientations had surfaced, and outside powers were drawn into this conflict. This
volatile mix of issues and tactics—geopolitical, religious, and national identity,
inviting intervention of outside parties, maneuvering to maintain power, and
inciting communal animosity—would continue to characterize Lebanon's civil
conflict and eventually lead to an all-out war. Perhaps as a result of this crisis, the
terms of General Shihab (1958-64) and his hand-picked successor Charles Helou
(1964-70) were distinguished by relatively less overt sectarian conflict.
Nevertheless, since the underlying divisive political structure was unchanged,
rivalry persisted between the sects (and within each sect) over control of state
power.

Impact of Regional Politics
The defeat of Egyptian, Syrian and Jordanian armies in the 1967 war was
followed by a period of Palestinian guerrilla attacks on Israel, mainly Lebanese
territory. Consistent with its policy of swift and harsh retaliation, Israel bombed
Beirut airport in December 1968, destroying thirteen civilian aircraft. The raid,
which was unanimously condemned by the U.N. Security Council, led to a political
crisis in Lebanon. While Muslim leaders proclaimed support for the Palestinian
cause, Christian leaders expressed their opposition to dragging Lebanon into the
Middle East conflict. Since most Palestinians are Sunni Muslims, Christians feared
that the growing Palestinian military presence would strengthen the influence of
Muslims in Lebanese politics. Also, widespread lawlessness in guerrilla-controlled
areas antagonized some Lebanese, and Israeli attacks on Lebanese villages caused
casualties, damage, and harm to Maronite-owned business interests.

By 1968 it was widely acknowledged that, while having only minority representation in Parliament, Muslims outnumbered Christians, largely due to the higher rates of Christian emigration and the relatively higher Muslim birth rates. Muslims demanded several government changes: an end to the rule that reserved key positions for Maronites only;[4] the strengthening of positions reserved for Muslims, such as the office of the prime minister; a correcting of the unequal distribution of resources; the establishment of an adequate welfare system to provide for the growing "misery belt" around Beirut; and demonstrations of Lebanon's commitment to fight against Israel by strengthening the army and coordinating with the Palestine Liberation Organization (PLO).

When the Jordanian army pushed the PLO military factions out of Jordan in 1970, most of their surviving forces fled to refugee camps in south Lebanon, where Palestinian refugees had lived since the founding of Israel in 1948. From here the PLO increased its attacks on Israel and the occupied territories, and Israel responded by bombing and shelling Lebanese towns and villages. The relative autonomy the Lebanese government agreed to give to the PLO under the terms of the 1969 Cairo agreement was solidified by the newly arrived fighters from Jordan. Several Lebanese factions sought to use the PLO's autonomy and political and military power to press their demands for greater participation in the decision making.

Convinced that the government was too weak to contain the PLO, the Maronite groups took matters into their own hands and stepped up their violent campaign against Palestinian military presence. Combined attacks from Israeli forces and Maronite Phalange (the largest Maronite political party and militia), in addition to the government's hands-off policy, galvanized the Muslim/leftist/Palestinian alliance and gave long-simmering economic and political complaints encouragement.

In 1970, Sulaiman Franjieh, a conservative Maronite from the north, was elected president in a narrow vote. Realizing that pervasive restrictions on free expression had contributed to the violent tenor of the opposition, Franjieh attempted to arrest the slide towards communal warfare by easing radio and television censorship and legalizing some banned radical parties. These modest improvements might have been effective if implemented sooner and as part of a broader program of reform; as it was, unrest continued. The government used force to suppress workers' strikes protesting unemployment and inflation, and students' demonstrations against perceived government collusion with the U.S.,

---

[4] In addition to the presidency, the commander of the army and the governor of the central bank were positions reserved for Maronites.

Israel, the Phalanges and conservative Arab regimes. Palestinian attacks against Israel intensified and Lebanese southern villages bore the brunt of Israel's often-indiscriminate retaliation. Thousands fled north seeking safety, causing an internal migration crisis that both weakened Lebanese agriculture, which was then the nation's largest employer, and increased pressure in Beirut's southern suburbs (the misery belt) populated by predominantly poor and displaced Shi`a from the south.

During the early 1970s, the Lebanese government's attempts to limit attacks on Israel from the south led to armed clashes between the army and the PLO and some Muslim factions. The October 1973 Arab-Israeli war led to an escalation of the fighting, further depopulating the area and fueling opposition to the political system dominated by Maronite and Sunni elites.

Start of the Civil War

Most Lebanese date the civil war from April 1975, when the Maronite Phalange fighters massacred thirty-six Palestinian occupants of a bus attempting to pass through a Maronite-dominated area. Following the massacre, communal violence erupted in full force.

The PLO abandoned its declared policy of non-interference in Lebanese politics ,and its several groups openly joined or supported the Muslim/leftist Lebanese side. The Lebanese army, which had long reflected the countries communal divisions, disintegrated along sectarian lines. Soldiers and army officers—sometimes whole units—joined the sectarian fighting on one side or the other. Predictably, Israel sided with the Maronite militias, while Syria initially appeared to be neutral. Saudi Arabia, Jordan and Egypt supported the Phalanges with money, arms and training facilities. By June, when the Maronite-based government was about to collapse, Syria sent its army to prop it up and soon afterwards the military balance shifted against the alliance of Muslim's, leftist's and Palestinians. As the violence escalated and engulfed the country, communities became more polarized and Lebanese from all groups found it nearly impossible to remain neutral. As militias swept through towns and villages, civilians—even those who felt no particular communal group identity—were forced, often literally at gunpoint, to choose a side in order to live. Communities that for years had co-existed peacefully, were caught up in the frenzied slaughter, fighting each other to survive. Hundreds of thousands were forced to flee their homes. Beirut, once the attractive flourishing business and cultural center of the Middle East was converted into a bombed out and dangerous urban war zone.

During the period between April 1975 and October 1976, over 50,000 were estimated to have been killed and 100,000 wounded; the overwhelming majority of victims were civilians.

Israel and the Palestinians

While the civil war was raging in 1976-78, Palestinian guerrillas and their Lebanese allies continued operations against Israel. The attacks gave the leftist/Muslim alliance a unifying ideology and political legitimacy. In March 1978, after a PLO attack left thirty-five civilians dead in Tel Aviv, Israel launched a ground, sea and air attack against Lebanon, killing or injuring thousands of civilians. Since then, despite U.N. Security Resolution 425 ordering withdrawal, Israel has maintained a significant military presence in southern Lebanon, with assistance from a proxy Lebanese militia.

In April 1979, Maj. Sa`ad Haddad, a Lebanese army officer, announced the formation of Independent Free Lebanon in areas under Israeli occupation in southern Lebanon. Ostensibly formed to safeguard Christian interests in the South, the militia which was later renamed South Lebanon Army (SLA) was financed, armed, trained by Israel. Its main function appeared to be assisting Israel's security operations.

The Israeli Invasion of 1982

The July 24, 1981 ceasefire between Israel and its adversaries in Lebanon lasted until June 1982, when Israel launched a massive land, sea and air attack on Lebanon following an assassination attempt on its London ambassador. While the main players in that summer campaign were Israel and the PLO, those events demonstrated the confluence of the various actors in the conflict. Jockeying for power and influence had started in earnest among Lebanese factions with an eye on the presidential elections that were scheduled for September 1982. The full-scale invasion delivered a crushing blow to the military power of the PLO and its Lebanese allies, decisively tipping the balance in favor of the Maronite minority, whose leaders were then poised to assume effective control of the government.

The invasion resulted in massive loss of life, estimated at 20,000 dead, mostly civilians. During the first two weeks of the invasion, 14,000 were reported killed, about 80 percent of them civilians. In Beirut alone, over 5,000 civilians were killed as a result of the daily heavy bombardment during a fifty-two-day siege laid by Israeli forces during July and August to eject PLO fighters from the city.

On August 23, Parliament chose Bashir Jemayel, the pro-Israel hardline head of the Phalanges, to be president. However, on September 14, he was assassinated before taking office, leading to widespread indiscriminate retaliation by his supporters. Although the suspects in the attack were later identified as members of the National Social Syrian Party, a predominantly Christian pro-Syrian political group, the retaliatory attacks mainly targeted Palestinians living in refugee camps in Beirut. Two days after the assassination, in one of the most gruesome incidents of the Lebanese conflict, a Phalange faction led by Elie Hobaiqa attacked the Palestinian refugee camps of Sabra and Shatila and massacred about 1,000 unarmed refugees, including children, women and old men.[5] The Israeli occupation forces, which contrary to a U.S.-brokered agreement had moved into Beirut the day after the assassination, were widely blamed for allowing the massacre to take place and not intervening to stop it once it had begun. After the massacre, Israeli forces withdrew from the city, redeployed to Beirut airport and consolidated their positions in the south.[6]

Parliament reconvened on September 21 and chose Amin Jemayel, Bashir's older brother, for president. Although the new president was less distrusted by the Muslim/leftist alliance, the alliance's battle with the Maronite militias survived the Israeli invasion. During the remainder of 1982, clashes continued in the Shouf between pro-Syrian Socialist Progressive Party (the main Druze militia) and the Lebanese Forces/Phalange militias, Israel's main allies.[7] Under U.S. pressure, Israel and Lebanon agreed to negotiate an end to Israeli occupation of most of Lebanon.[8] A U.S.- brokered agreement, doomed without Syrian support, was signed on May 17. Israel conditioned its own acceptance on Syria's willingness to withdraw. Syria's allies in Lebanon, grouped under the National Salvation Front, eventually defeated the May 17 agreement,[9] after which

---

[5] Hobaiqa, now considered an ally of Syria, is currently minister of electricity in the Hariri government. In October 1990, he led a Maronite faction in support of the Lebanese and Syrian armies' action to oust the rebel Gen. Michel Aoun. Hobaiqa's group, at the time part of the Lebanese Forces, was implicated in gross abuses in the areas that came under its control.

[6] At the time, Israel's allies controlled parts of the south and substantial parts of Mount Lebanon, while in the rest of the country, Syria and its allies were in control.

[7] Meanwhile, in the northern city of Tripoli, fighting erupted between pro-Syrian Communist militants and anti-Syrian Sunni Islamists.

[8] A February 22, 1983 suggestion by President Reagan to provide U.S. guarantees for Israel's northern border instead of an actual Israeli presence in Lebanon was rejected by the Israeli government.

[9] The newly formed front included Maronite leaders sympathetic to Syria, especially former President Sulaiman Franjieh and Prime Minister Rashid Karami, in addition to Druze and Shi`a militias. Faced with this opposition and Syria's pressure, the Lebanese government withdrew its support of the May 17 agreement.

Israel's sphere of influence was limited to the self-declared security zone, which it continues to occupy.

This final diplomatic failure crushed the last bit of hope of some Lebanese that the Israeli invasion—by dramatically shifting the balance of power—would bring an end to Lebanon's communal violence. But foreign powers, like Lebanon's communal and government leaders, were more interested in controlling the country than resolving its conflicts. When they were denied the control, they usually ensured that no other party would win out. And while each community, on its own, was too weak to seize and hold onto power, all were strong enough to wreck each others attempts.

The Role of Syria

After Israel's withdrawal from most of the Lebanese territory it overran in the 1982 invasion, Syria launched a campaign through its proxies to secure control of the country. A "national front" was formed in August by leaders allied with Syria, who were allowed to attack their opponents and enlarge their areas of control. In 1985, over 500 civilians were killed in Tripoli and 500,000 displaced. The fighting stopped when the Syrian army moved into the city. At the same time, Syria urged its allies to conclude a new national pact, under which the country would be run by a six-party council representing six major sects and a 198-seat parliament divided equally between Christians and Muslims. The plan called for the president to be Maronite, but for some of his traditional powers to be relegated to the prime minister, who would be Muslim. The plan explicitly recognized the "common interests" between Syria and Lebanon and called for "strategic integration" in defense, internal security and foreign policy.

The plan was strongly opposed by Hizballa, a major Shi'a party supported by Iran, the Sunni militia al-Murabitoun, and Christian leaders not allied with Syria, including President Jemayel. Druze leader Jumblat withdrew his support as he realized that the plan would reduce his autonomy, leaving the Shi'a party, Amal, as the only major supporter of the accord. Rejection of the Syrian-sponsored agreement resulted in government paralysis; in January 1986, bloody sectarian clashes resumed.

When Syria's allies could not prevail by themselves, the Syrian army joined the fight. In June 1986, Syrian troops moved into West Beirut. In February 1987 war broke out in West Beirut between the pro-Syrian mainly Shi'a Amal militia and a front formed between the Druze, Communist Party and Sunni Murabitoun militias. Syria moved in 7,000 additional troops to stop the fighting and close down seventy-five militia offices in that part of the city.

In September 1988, when President Jemayel's term expired, Lebanon's rigid sectarian system broke down under the pressure of competing communities. After attempts to find a successor acceptable to all factions failed, Jemayel took the unprecedented step of appointing a Maronite (Pierre Helou) to head the government from the position of prime minister. The idea was immediately rejected as a violation of the National Pact, which mandated that the prime minister be a Sunni Muslim. Jemayel then decided to appoint a military council headed by Gen. Michael Aoun, another Maronite, to run the country. The civilian cabinet headed by Selim al-Hoss, a Sunni, rejected the decision as unconstitutional. For two years, with the political system incapable of pulling the country out of crisis, Lebanon continued to have dual governments, each claiming legitimacy.

General Aoun's attempt to establish army control of Beirut badly backfired. In March 1989, he declared his intention to rid Lebanon of all foreign forces, including those of Syria. While most Lebanese probably supported this goal, targeting Syria by name proved to be a fatal mistake. During March and April, clashes and artillery duels between the Lebanese army and Syrian forces occurred almost daily. In early 1989, Iraq emerged as a new source of support for Aoun. Having signed a truce with Iran, Saddam Hussein used the Lebanon battleground to settle his account with Syria's Asad, his long time rival. Iraq poured money and weapons into Lebanon, prolonging the fighting and increasing the casualties, but unable to change the outcome.

Taif Accord

In an attempt to address the underlying causes of the conflict, including issues of succession, elections and political reform, the Arab League adopted its long-awaited plan for peace in Lebanon in September 1989. In addition to an "immediate and comprehensive" ceasefire to be supervised by the Arab League, the plan called for convening the Chamber of Deputies to discuss the "charter of reconciliation" drafted by the league's representatives. Syria endorsed the plan, which did not call for the withdrawal of Syrian troops. The Arab League plan was also endorsed by France, the Soviet Union, the U.K. and the U.S. Aoun grudgingly accepted the ceasefire, which took effect on September 23, but rejected the plan.

On September 30, the Arab League Plan, hereafter referred to as the Taif Accord, was signed in the Saudi resort city of Taif. The sixty-two Lebanese members of parliament—85 percent of the surviving seventy-three members—who met in Saudi Arabia included thirty-one Christian and thirty-one Muslim deputies. On October 22, the parliament formally adopted the accord, with fifty-eight out of sixty-two members present voting for it. The accord shifted some executive power from the president to the prime minister and the cabinet, which was to be divided equally between Christians and Muslims. The president appoints the prime minister, who in turn chooses members of his cabinet in consultation with the president. The other significant change was to divide parliamentary seats equally between Christians and Muslims, with fixed percentages for each sect within the two major religions.[10] All of these changes were to be temporary, until Parliament was able to reconsider the sectarian basis of government. According to the Taif Accord, Syrian forces were to remain in Lebanon for a maximum of two years to assist the Lebanese government in implementing the security plan.

Aoun rejected the Taif Accord as an infringement on Lebanon's sovereignty—a position tacitly supported by mainstream groups, such as the Phalanges. On November 5, Parliament chose Rene Mou`awwadh, a pro-Syrian Maronite, to be the next president, but he was assassinated seventeen days later. Soon after the election, Aoun declared it unconstitutional and called for the "dissolution" of Parliament. On November 24, Parliament reconvened and chose Elias el-Hrawi, another pro-Syrian Maronite, to replace him. Predictably, Aoun rejected el-Hrawi as a Syrian puppet and continued his defiance.

On January 31, 1990, after the Lebanese Forces, led by Samir Ja`ja`, announced its reluctant endorsement of the Taif Accord, Aoun declared war against the group, hitherto his main ally, and attacked its strongholds in the Christian heartland. Before the fighting stopped in mid-March, nearly 750 civilians were killed and 3,000 wounded, but the Lebanese Forces continued to support the new accord.

The End of the Civil War

Foreign powers frequently supported one religious sect against the other. But in several cases within each sect there were factions supported by different governments. For example, within the Shi'a sect, there have been several factions: while Amal was supported by Syria and Hizballa by Iran, several Shi'a leaders supported traditional Maronite leaders. The rank and file of the Communist Party, sported by the Soviet Union, were Shi'a, as well as many of the rank and file (and some officers) of Israeli-supported South Lebanon Army. Similarly, while the Marada Maronite militia was openly supported by Syria, the Lebanese Forces, also Maronite, were armed by Israel. Sunni leaders were divided among Saudi

---

[10] The Taif Accord increased the number of seats from ninety-nine to 108, which was later raised to 128 divided as follows. On the Muslim side, twenty-seven were allocated to Sunnis, twenty-seven for Shi`a, eight for Druze and two for Alawis; on the Christian side thirty-four were allocated to Maronites, fourteen for Greek Orthodox, eight for Greek Catholics, five for Armenian Orthodox and one each for Armenian Catholics, Protestants and other Christian sects.

supporters, Libya loyalists, Soviet-backed and Iraq partisans. Orthodox Christian leaders dominated the Syrian national Social Popular Party, a pro-Syrian group, while others were prominent in the Communist Party leadership.

Much of the fighting that took place within some sects following the Taif Accord appeared to be directly over control of power and representation in the new regime. In addition to the intra-Maronite fighting in early 1990, intra-Shi`a conflict flared up again. The Gulf crisis, which started on August 2 with the invasion of Kuwait, directly affected the fighting in Lebanon by depriving Aoun of his chief supplier of arms, money and political support—Iraq's Saddam Hussein. Emboldened by the isolation of its rival and by its membership in the U.S.-led alliance formed to evict Saddam Hussein from Kuwait, the Syrian government's hand was strengthened in Lebanon.

Its first step was to expedite implementation of the Taif Accord. On August 21, the Chamber of Deputies adopted wide-ranging constitutional amendments based on the accord. In addition to increasing the number of parliamentary seats to 108 divided equally between Christians and Muslims, amendments included strengthening parliamentary rule. Dissolving the parliament, which had been a prerogative of the president, was made more difficult. The position of Parliament speaker was given more power and its term was extended to four years, instead of merely one year. By most standards, the office of prime minister, whose co-signature was now required for nearly all presidential decisions, was the main beneficiary of the reapportionment of executive power. The prime minister's co-signature was now required for nearly all presidential decisions. While the president retained the title of commander-in-chief, the army was put under authority of the council of ministers, in which the president no longer had a vote.

The defeat of General Aoun in October 1990 signalled the end of the final round in the civil war. Syria and its allies were in firm control of most of Lebanon. On December 24, a new "government of national reconciliation" was formed and charged with implementing the Taif Accord. The new cabinet, headed by Omar Karami, a pro-Syrian Sunni, was composed of thirty ministers representing most militias and religious and political groups, with the notable exception of Hizballa. Criticizing Syrian influence, the Lebanese Forces and Phalanges soon began a boycott of the cabinet and in January, Walid Jumblat, the Druze leader, resigned. But the government survived, and by the spring, as the Gulf war wound down, the critics returned to attending cabinet meetings. The army began to disarm militias of their heavy weapons. Only Hizballa, regarded as necessary to balance the Israeli-backed South Lebanon Army, was spared.

Post-War Restructuring

As it recovers from fifteen years of civil war, the Lebanese government appears to have three main reconstruction objectives: preserving sectarian privileges, disarming militias and strengthening the security forces to keep the peace. In the belief that basic freedoms threaten this fragile process, they have been circumscribed. The government frequently prosecutes journalists, closes newspapers, dissolves peaceful associations, and bans public assembly.

Because prosecution of civil war crimes was considered a potentially explosive issue, Parliament passed a sweeping amnesty for most civil war crimes committed before March 28, 1991. Excluded were massacres, assassinations, and attempted assassinations of political leaders, religious figures and diplomats. Although a number of senior officials, including members of the current cabinet, had been leaders of militias implicated in such crimes, they have not been investigated. Neither the killings of nearly 200,000 during the war or the disappearances of about 14,000 persons—virtually all civilians—were investigated. Despite repeated demands by families of the missing, the government has failed to mount a serious search for those who were kidnapped and subsequently disappeared during the civil war.

Although the disarming of militias was described by the government as generally successful, events later indicated that the success was more apparent than real. Hizballa and the Iranian Revolutionary Guards[11] were not disarmed at all. Other militias were given ample time to remove their weapons to the Israeli-occupied security zone or deep into sectarian-held areas, beyond the reach of the government's feeble forces. Some militias sold arms in the black market.[12]

Nearly five years after the signing of the Taif Accord officially ended the civil war the government continues to hod out the threat of a return to communal violence to justify its repressive restrictions on the free exercise of civil and political rights. It has frequently argued that "excessive freedom" may plunge the country back into the morass of civil war. However, these restrictions appear to be part of a concerted and deliberate policy to stifle the opposition and strengthen those in power in the name of stemming the threat of civil war. Instead of

---

[11] Iranian irregulars supported by the Iranian government, the Iranian Revolutionary Guards are based mainly in the Beqa' Valley providing training and logistical support for Hizballa.

[12] In June 1994, Lebanese authorities disclosed that Ghassan Touma, a senior officer in the Lebanese Forces security division, had been involved in selling substantial amounts of the Forces' weapons to the Bosnian Serbs.

contributing to peaceful coexistence between Lebanon's diverse religious and ethnic groups, these restrictions will most likely worsen the political and economic crisis in Lebanon. By closing down outlets for nonviolent opposition, Lebanon may be encouraging dissidents to return to the violent and lawless methods of the civil-war period.

While the Lebanese government's stated concerns over the possible resumption of the disastrous civil war are of course understandable, it is not clear that the root causes are being addressed. The Taif Accords promise to reconsider, and eventually do away with, the confessionally-based system has been largely abandoned. Instead of addressing the divisive state structure which engenders conflict, the government has chosen strategies that may in fact fuel strife. Merely increasing the number of parliamentary seats and redividing them to reflect the current sizes of Lebanon's fifteen sects may address some of group demands, but it fails to take into account individual rights. It is difficult to see how restricting peaceful dissent may have a positive effect. On the contrary, as such restrictions have aroused suspicions about the government's desire to conduct dialogue with its opponents, they may, in fact, lead to heightening tensions among Lebanon's diverse communities. Censorship appears to have been used to safeguard the immediate interests of President Elias Hrawi and his family, protecting from criticism Prime Minister Rafiq Hariri and the policies of his government, and guarding the interests of Syria and Saudi Arabia.

Contrary to the government's claims that restrictions of civil and political rights can help contain impulses to wage civil war, there is no evidence that such measures in the past ever arrested Lebanon's descent into chaos. For example, in 1977, the Lebanese government dealt the severest blows to press freedom when it imposed pre-publication censorship, gave security forces wide-ranging authority to muzzle the press, and issued the most stringent post-publication censorship regulation limiting what the press may publish and stiffening punishment for infractions. Despite those steps, the war intensified. Similarly, Amin Jemayel's attempts in 1983 to silence media critics were followed by an escalation of the war.[13] In fact, a review of Lebanon's history shows that attacks on basic liberties, which went largely unpunished, preceded periods of intense civil strife and might have helped precipitate them. Government policies restricting basic freedoms have failed to prevent a resumption of civil war practices; politically motivated killings and abductions resumed, with apparent impunity.

---

[13] Further discussion of the restrictions imposed by Decree 104 and their effects may be found in Human Rights Watch/Middle East, *Lebanon's Lively Press Faces Worst Crackdown Since 1976* (New York: Human Rights Watch, July 1993).

Conclusion

The many and diverse communities of Lebanon, pulled into a nation by outside powers, desperately needed a government that would act as an agent of integration, engendering a unifying national spirit; while protecting the rights of individuals, especially those in minority groups. The sectarian-based government structure, which might have been originally conceived as a formula to ensure equity, became, instead, a rigid structure that reinforced divisions by assigning positions and power according to religion. Political differences, which could only be expressed through the established polarized system, were colored by religion and manipulated by power hungry leaders or similarly self interested foreign governments.

The promise of the Taif Accords to reconsider the confessional basis of the system appears to have been forgotten. There has been little discussion of this issue in Parliament and most indications are that it is not expected to be raised in the near future. In respect to election district design, there has been an actual reversal of a Taif Accord reform. In an attempt to lessen sectarian divisions, the accord had stipulated that elections be held at the provincial level, in place of district-level contests that were common in the prewar period. But the election regulations adopted by the Hrawi government in 1992 included several provisions which strengthened its influence over the outcome. For example, in certain provinces, district-level elections were maintained, apparently to improve election prospects for pro-government candidates, despite the fact that this gerrymandering also heightened sectarian resentment.[14]

Groups marginalized by the newly restructured system may resort to violence to achieve their goals if they are denied peaceful means. Banning public assembly, dissolving peaceful associations, closing newspapers and other news organizations, and most recently banning the broadcasting of news and political commentary narrow the margin allowed for peaceful dissent.

Lebanon's state structure was respected only when it was seen as an honest broker between competing groups and individuals. When it favored certain groups or individuals over others, the aggrieved parties' trust in the government waned. Individuals and groups must be allowed to detect shifts and peacefully call for the correction of the imbalances, whether real or perceived.

Muzzling dissent in the name of reconciliation is a cynical attempt to exploit the fear of a relapse into civil war. These tactics serve to maintain the status quo of state structure, which in Lebanon benefits only small groups of

---

[14] For more details, see Human Rights Watch, *World Report 1993* (New York: Human Rights Watch, 1992), p. 328.

leaders and their followers, leaving the unaffiliated—perhaps the majority—unrepresented and under-served.

ARMENIA-AZERBAIJAN

Centuries of hatred. Blood enemies. Intractable religious animosity. All have been used to describe the conflict between Christian Armenians and Muslim Azeris[1] over the Nagorno-Karabakh Autonomous Oblast,[2] a mountainous, Armenian-populated enclave wedged in Azerbaijan's southwest corner on the border with Armenia.[3] The current unrest began in 1988, as Armenian national groups both in Nagorno-Karabakh and Armenia proper began a campaign for a union of the two areas. The campaign which began with demonstrations led to bloodshed and violence between Azeris and Armenians, and by 1992 the violence had become a full-scale war. In 1993, the war outgrew Nagorno-Karabakh itself, with almost all the fighting spilling over into Azerbaijan proper as Karabakh Armenian forces[4]—often with the support of forces from the Republic of Armenia—conducted large-scale operations that resulted in the seizure of all the Azeri-populated provinces surrounding Nagorno-Karabakh on the south, west, and

---

[1]Throughout, "Azeri" will refer to those who are ethnically Azeri, such as an "Azeri woman" or an "Azeri-populated village." "Azerbaijani" will refer to organizations connected with the Republic of Azerbaijan, such as the "Azerbaijani Army." This division is arbitrary and limited to this report.

[2]Although the Nagorno-Karabakh Autonomous Oblast of Azerbaijan declared independence in January 1992 as the Republic of Nagorno-Karabakh, no country recognizes this independence, and under international law the area remains part of Azerbaijan. In this report, "Nagorno-Karabakh" refers to the Nagorno-Karabakh Autonomous Oblast.

[3]Before violence broke out in 1988, approximately 40,000 Azeris lived in Nagorno-Karabakh out of a population of 185,000. Today all have been ejected. In addition, the roughly 160,000 Azeris who lived in Armenia fled to Azerbaijan by 1989, and Azerbaijan's Armenian community of roughly 350,000 left Azerbaijan after anti-Armenian pogroms in 1988 and 1990. Today a few Armenians, most of mixed marriage or descent, still live in Baku.

[4]The war in Nagorno-Karabakh presents a particularly complex case for the use of ethnic identifiers. "Karabakh Armenians" is used to signify forces connected with the self-proclaimed, breakaway "Republic of Nagorno-Karabakh." "Karabakh Armenian" forces, however, may include citizens of the Republic of Armenia, mercenaries, and members of the armed forces of the Republic of Armenia. Only where it can be determined that soldiers in an action are overwhelmingly from the armed forces of the Republic of Armenia will the term "Armenian forces" or "Armenian soldiers" be used.

east[5] and in the forcible displacement of the Azeri civilian population. An estimated 25,000 have been killed and over one million displaced in this conflict. Today, Azeri farmers no longer till Armenian soil, and Armenians have vanished from the streets of Baku, Azerbaijan's capital. The Azeri mosque in Shusha and the Armenian church in Baku stand empty.

This transpired not because Armenians and Azeris are fundamentally incapable of living at peace with each other. Rather, it evolved in the context of Soviet government inaction and incompetence in the face of ethnic tensions between Armenians and Azeris. The Soviet government might have stemmed anti-Armenian violence in Azerbaijan in 1988 and 1990, well before war broke out. Instead, it merely used ethnic tensions as a pretext to crack down on the Azerbaijani independence movement. In 1991, Soviet military actions in Nagorno-Karabakh, carried out jointly with Azerbaijani troops, contributed greatly to the intensification of armed conflict in Nagorno-Karabakh.

As full-scale war broke out, systematic abuse of human rights was carried out by Karabakh Armenian forces and by the governments of Azerbaijan and Armenia. In 1992, while the Azerbaijan military held a strategic advantage in Nagorno-Karabakh, it bombed and shelled civilian targets, took hostages and mistreated the civilian population. Because 1993 witnessed unrelenting Karabakh Armenian offensives against the Azerbaijani provinces surrounding Nagorno-Karabakh,[6] most of the violations during this period were the direct result of these offensive actions.[7] Karabakh Armenian violations of human rights include forced displacement of the Azeri population by means of indiscriminate and targeted shelling of civilian populations, capture of civilian stragglers, the taking and holding of hostages; the mistreatment and likely summary execution of prisoners of war and other captives; and the looting and burning of civilian homes. Some

---

[5]Karabakh Armenian forces currently occupy 20 to 25 percent of Azerbaijan.

[6]In 1993, Nagorno-Karabakh Armenian forces captured the following provinces of Azerbaijan: Kelbajar, Agdam, Qubatli, Jebrayil, Fizuli and Zangelan. They also captured part of Agjebed province and Lachin province. While Azeri forces launched a massive offensive in the latter part of December 1993, all the fighting took place in Azerbaijan proper and over areas already emptied of their civilian populations.

[7]Whichever side is on the offensive forces out the civilian population and loots and destroys homes and other civilian objects. Azerbaijani forces exhibited similar behavior during their June 1992 offensive against Mardakert province in Nagorno-Karabakh.

instances of looting and pillaging, such as in Agdam, an Azeri city of some 50,000 that fell to Karabakh Armenian forces in July 1993, were organized and planned by the authorities of Nagorno-Karabakh. Azerbaijani violations during this period include indiscriminate use of air power resulting in civilian casualties; hostage-taking; and the mistreatment and likely execution of prisoners.

Since late 1993, the conflict has also clearly become internationalized: in addition to Azerbaijani and Karabakh Armenian forces, troops from the Republic of Armenia participate on the Karabakh side in fighting inside Azerbaijan and in Nagorno-Karabakh. The Republic of Armenia's violations include holding hostages; and the likely killing of prisoners of war. Foreign mercenaries hired by all sides have also been responsible for widespread violations of human rights.[8]

Background

The area comprising Nagorno-Karabakh was ceded by the Persian Empire to the Russian Empire in 1813. Tsarist policies radically altered the ethnic composition of the newly conquered territory by encouraging Armenians to immigrate from the Ottoman and Persian empires. Christian Armenian farmers, for example, were encouraged to settle in border areas with Ottoman Turkey and Persia to serve as a buffer.[9] While Armenians had always lived in Azerbaijan—and Eastern Armenia was their historic home—waves of Muslim invaders and centuries of war between the Ottoman and Persian empires had reduced their numbers greatly in the period preceding Russia conquest in 1828.[10]

---

[8]Afghan "mujahideen" and Slavic mercenaries also take part in the fighting.

[9] A similar phenomenon can be seen in the Krajina, the Serb-belt in Croatia straddling Bosnia-Herzegovina's northern border. The Hapsburgs encouraged Serb settlement in the area, which at the time was the border with the Ottoman Empire. The one difference is that Eastern Armenia had been home to Armenians before the Tsar encouraged their immigration in the nineteenth century; the same is not true of Serbs in the Krajina.

[10]George A. Baibournoutian, "The Ethnic Composition and the Socio-Economic Conditions of Eastern Armenia in the First Half of the Nineteenth Century," in *Transcaucasia: Nationalism and Social Change* (Ann Arbor, Michigan: Michigan Slavic Publications, 1983), pp. 69-86. While it appears that Eastern Armenia had an Armenian majority until the mid-fourteenth century, shortly after 1830 they numbered roughly 20 percent of the population. Pockets of Armenian settlement might have existed where the Armenian percentage of the population exceeded 20 percent. Nagorno-Karabakh may have been one such area, though no census data exist for the time of Russian conquest,

While Tsarist demographic manipulation was problematic, its communal favoritism was especially harmful. With few exceptions, Tsarist colonial rule favored Christian Armenians over Muslim Azerbaijanis.[11] Russia's pro-Armenian policy expressed itself in numerous ways. With his Edict ("Polozheniye") of 1836, Tsar Nicholas I (1825-55) granted the Armenian Church institutional autonomy, namely the right to run its churches and schools largely unhindered.[12] Muslim religious authorities enjoyed no such autonomy; they suffered under state regulation, and attempts were made at conversion.[13] The civil service was largely Armenian, though their higher education levels could explain this. Consequently, Armenians were often viewed by Azeris as surrogates for the Russian state.[14] Until 1908, regulations under the Urban Reform of 1870 prevented Muslims in Baku from holding more than one-third of the seats on the city council though as property owners they constituted 80 percent of the electorate.[15] Finally, although there were several wealthy and influential Azerbaijani notables and merchants, an iron-clad labor hierarchy held sway: Europeans at the top; Armenians and Russians in the middle; Muslims at the bottom.[16]

---

before Armenian immigration.

[11]One of those exceptions was Governor General of Transcaucasia Prince Grigorii Golitsyn from 1896-1903. His rule favored Azerbaijanis.

[12]Ronald Grigor Suny, *Looking Toward Ararat: Armenia and Modern History* (Bloomington: Indiana University Press, 1993), p. 40.

[13]Audrey Altstadt, *The Azerbaijani Turks: Power and Identity under Russian Rule* (Stanford, California: Hoover Institute Press, 1992), p. 19.

[14]Ibid., p. 40.

[15]Ibid., p. 25. In 1908 Azeris defied the law and took a majority of seats on the council. The Russian viceroy offered only mild protest, and the council remained majority Azeri until the Russian Revolution.

[16]Ronald Grigor Suny, "The Revenge of the Past: Socialism and Ethnic Conflict in Transcaucasia," *New Left Review*, No. 184 (New York, 1990), p. 17.

The growing sense of nationalism among Armenians in Transcaucasia[17] in the late nineteenth century clashed head on—in the person of Governor General of Transcaucasia Prince Grigorii Golitsyn (1896-1903)—with Russian aims at centralization. Golitsyn reversed traditional pro-Armenian policies, reducing the number of Armenians in the civil service and replacing them with Azeris. He also closed Armenian schools and, in 1903, ordered the confiscation of Armenian church property.[18] At the same time, the governor general allowed Azeris to open newspapers and to conduct certain courses in the high schools in Azeri.

After the outbreak of the Russian revolution in 1905, the newly founded republics of Armenia and Azerbaijan fought bitterly for control of Nagorno-Karabakh, with British troops briefly occupying the enclave. Transcaucasia exploded in violence during the revolution, as long-simmering communal tensions, labor unrest, and revolutionary activity all reached a critical mass. Between February and November 1905, the violence encompassed Yerevan, Nakhichevan, Shusha, Tbilisi, and Ganja. An estimated 155 Azeri and 128 Armenian villages were destroyed and 3,000 to 10,000 people were killed.[19]

Many scholars point to a Tsarist hand in the conflict: local authorities, short of troops because of the Russo-Japanese War, may have intentionally inflamed hostility between Christian Armenians and Muslim Azeris to weaken resistance against the Russian government. In January 1905, for example, Prince V.I. Nakashidze, governor of Baku, authorized a large number of weapons permits for Muslims.[20] Police authorities did little to end violence. The caprice of official policy also destabilized the situation. After Prince Vorontsov-Dashkov was appointed viceroy of the Caucasus in May 1905, the traditional pro-Armenian policy was reinstated and Russian troops were given orders to shoot at Azeri crowds.

---

[17]The term "Transcaucasia" is a Russian notion. The term refers to the land mass south of the Caucasus mountains, seen from a northern (Russian) perspective: modern day Georgia, Azerbaijan, and Armenia. In Russian, "Zakavkaz'e" literally translates as "beyond the Caucasus."

[18]Tadeusz Swietochowksi, *Russian Azerbaijan, 1905-1920: The Shaping of National Identity in a Muslim Community* (Cambridge and New York: Cambridge University Press, 1985), p. 40.

[19]Ibid., p. 41.

[20]Ibid.

Russia's Romanov dynasty collapsed under the weight of the First World War, and Azerbaijan and Armenia both declared independent republics. These were short-lived states that by 1920 were reincorporated into the Russian/Soviet fold. During this brief interlude, ethnic tensions flared again fueled by greater political goals. In March 1918, in an effort to seize Baku from local Muslim forces, Soviet Bolsheviks made a pact with the Armenian nationalist Dashnak party. In an orgy of violence that followed, between 3,000 and 3,500 Muslims were massacred.[21] Less than six months later, in September 1918, the Ottoman "Army of Islam" supported by local Azeri forces recaptured Baku. This time an estimated 10,000 Armenians were slaughtered. As the "Great Game" was played out over Transcaucasia and British, Ottoman, Bolshevik, Azerbaijani, and Armenian forces criss-crossed the region, thousands more innocent Armenians and Azeris would lose their lives in communal violence.[22] In 1921, after the imposition of Soviet power in Transcaucasia, the Bolsheviks awarded Nagorno-Karabakh to Azerbaijan in a decision hotly contested by Armenians.

During the Soviet period under the slogan "National in form, Socialist in content," non-Russian nationalities enjoyed limited expression in certain aspects of life, such as culture, but most political, social, and economic life was subordinated to the center, namely to the Communist Party in Moscow. For example, ethnic folk dancing was approved, whereas questioning the exploitation of natural resources or the allocation of housing was not. Within this paradigm, there were the ebbs and flows of Soviet policy: the 1920s witnessed a brief flourishing of "national communists," while the 1930s ushered in Stalinist purges of "bourgeois nationalists." By the 1970s, the talk was of the "new Soviet man" and the "merging of nations": shorthand for the rise of a Russified, Russophone Soviet citizenry.[23] Then under Gorbachev, "perestroika," and the response to it on the part of long-repressed national groups, forced the nationalities question to reappear on the Soviet agenda.

The "Nagorno-Karabakh question" occupied the foremost spot on that

---

[21]Altstadt, *The Azerbaijani Turks*, pp. 85-87 ; Suny, "The Revenge of the Past," p. 29.

[22] See Richard Hovannisian, "The Armeno-Azerbaijani Conflict over Mountainous Nagorno-Karabakh, 1918-1919," *Armenian Review*, Summer 1971). Hovannisian's article outlines the policy fluctuations of the British troops garrisoned in the area. Initially they supported Armenian interests, than switched to favor the Azeris.

[23]"Sliyaniye Narodov," literally the fusing together of peoples.

agenda. Since the early 1920s, when Joseph Stalin and the Caucasian Buro had awarded Nagorno-Karabakh to Azerbaijan after it had been granted to Armenia, Armenians living in Nagorno-Karabakh claimed discrimination from Azerbaijani authorities in Baku.[24]

In 1988, when Armenians demanded the unification of Nagorno-Karabakh with Armenia proper, their demands triggered a chain reaction of violence. Pogroms in Sumgait, Azerbaijan, in February 1988 had claimed at least thirty-two lives, mostly Armenian. Large rallies and small scale violence had broken out intermittently over the next two years. The Soviet military from time to time had ruled over Yerevan and Baku, and in 1989 Moscow took direct control of Nagorno-Karabakh. Azerbaijan placed a trade embargo on Armenia, cutting off fuel. Under pressure, most Azerbaijanis fled Armenia, and large numbers of Armenians left Azerbaijan. By 1990, a virtual state of war existed between Armenia and Azerbaijan over Nagorno-Karabakh. During these critical two years, decaying Soviet institutions and the often inflammatory actions of Azerbaijani and Armenian populist groups contributed little in bringing about a peaceful resolution of the conflict. Soviet government actions, meanwhile, were largely detrimental and self-serving. Preserving Soviet power, rather than a concern for keeping the peace among Azerbaijan and Armenia, seemed to motivate Soviet policy.

The two most glaring examples of early prejudicial Soviet government action that resulted in intensified violence between Armenians and Azeris were "Black January" and "Operation Ring." "Black January," the bloody, violent suppression of the political opposition by Soviet troops in Baku, Azerbaijan in January 1990, left over one hundred, mostly Azeri civilians dead. In "Operation Ring," a spring/summer 1991 operation, Soviet army troops helped Azerbaijani Ministry of Interior forces deport Armenian civilians, mainly from the Shaumian region of Azerbaijan. "Operation Ring" became a turning-point in the Karabakh conflict, triggering full-scale war.

"Black January"
By January 1990, Azerbaijan, and especially its capital, Baku, were in turmoil. Large rallies by the Azerbaijani Popular Front, the main opposition group,

---

[24]Nagorno-Karabakh Armenian complaints concerning Azeri rule are in Gerard Libaridian's (ed) *The Nagorno-Karabakh File* (Cambridge and Toronto: Zoryan Institute, 1988). The main Armenian complaint seems to be undermining of Nagorno-Karabakh's autonomy by central authorities in Baku. For example, a wine factory that should have been under the direction of Nagorno-Karabakh authorities in Stepanakert, the enclave's capital, was actually under the authority of a nearby Azerbaijani city.

crowded Baku's streets. The rhetoric of these gatherings was heavily anti-Armenian. On January 13, 1990, a second set of anti-Armenian pogroms convulsed the city, taking forty-eight lives.[25]

While the government did not instigate these pogroms, central authorities, including the local militia and 12,000 Soviet Ministry of Interior troops in Baku, did little to stop the violence; they mostly occupied themselves with protecting Communist Party and government buildings. Various excuses were put forward to explain the inaction: the troops were not equipped to handle civil disorders; no orders were given; confusion in the chain of command. Some journalists pointed towards a conspiracy.[26]

After states of emergency were declared on January 15 in other parts of Azerbaijan—but surprisingly not in Baku—the pogrom activity started to subside. Waves of Armenian refugees, the majority of the 27,000 Armenians left in Baku after the 1988 pogroms, left the country.[27] Fearing Soviet military intervention, Azerbaijani Popular Front activists began a blockade of military barracks.

On the night of January 19, 1990, Soviet forces, under the authority of a state of emergency decree that would only be announced hours later, stormed Baku in an effort to crush the anti-Moscow Azerbaijani Popular Front and safeguard the rule of the Azerbaijani Communist Party. The Popular Front had taken *de facto* control in a number of Azerbaijani regions and was poised to win Supreme Soviet Elections scheduled for March 1990. While the Kremlin's ostensible reason for the military action was to safeguard the Armenian population, most evidence simply does not support this contention. For example, documents of the military procurator's office in Baku examined by Human Rights Watch/Helsinki indicate that the military action was being planned even before the January 13, 1990 pogroms.

The Soviet forces' deployment in Baku on January 19, 1991 not only failed to stem anti-Armenian attacks, but also raised serious doubts about whether

---

[25]Human Rights Watch/Helsinki, *Conflict in the Soviet Union: Black January in Azerbaijan* (New York: Human Rights Watch, May 1991), p. 7. Almost all those killed were Armenian. The following section is written with material from this report unless otherwise cited.

[26]See Bill Keller, "Did Moscow Incite Azerbaijanis? Some See a Plot," *New York Times*, February 19, 1990, p. A8.

[27]Michael Dobbs, "War Refugees Pour Into Armenia," *Washington Post*, January 18, 1990, p.1.

the Soviets wished to stem that violence. The action resulted in over one hundred civilian, mostly Azeri, deaths because of the unjustified and excessive use of force. Troops machine-gunned civilian buses, crushed cars with armored vehicles, and sprayed civilian housing areas with machinegun fire. In concentrating its efforts only on maintaining the party's control, the Soviet government effectively sanctioned the violence against Armenians.

Civil liberties, critical to the fostering of tolerance, were the second victim. Meetings, demonstrations, and strikes were banned, and the media were subjected to censorship. The action did not even achieve its official goal: most Armenians fled Baku. Kirov Park, a pretty, leafy spot overlooking Baku Harbor once favored for family outings and strolling, became a martyrs' cemetery for the Azeri civilians killed.

Operation Ring represents another clear example of biased, manipulative behavior by Soviet authorities. As the Soviet Union was living out its last months, troops from the Azerbaijani Ministry of the Interior and the 23rd Division of the 4th Soviet Army carried out what ostensibly were passport checks along the Armenian-Azeri border and in Khanlar and Shaumian provinces in the spring and summer of 1991.[28] The intent was to disarm Armenian guerrilla groups (fedayeen) that had been operating in the area in defiance of an order to disband and disarm. However, Operation Ring did not restrict fedayeen disarmament. Rather, Soviet soldiers and units of the Azerbaijani Ministry of the Interior attacked populated Armenian villages in the area. Often, the village would be bombarded and the inhabitants forced out. Once surrounded, troops would enter the village, checking documents and beating civilians. Often, men were arrested on suspicion of weapons possession and taken away to prisons, where they faced further beatings. Some villages fought back.[29]

The villages of Chaikent in Khanlar (Getashen) province and Martunashen in Shaumian province—where there was armed resistance to Operation Ring—were especially hard hit. In operations that began at the end of April 1991, Soviet soldiers and Azerbaijani riot troops surrounded the villages, then forced out

---

[28]The latter two regions are north of Nagorno-Karabakh. Unless otherwise indicated, this section was written from material in *Bloodshed in the Caucasus: Escalation of the Armed Conflict in Nagorno-Karabakh* (New York: Human Rights Watch, September 1992). Most of the information is taken from Appendix I of that report.

[29]In one incident on April 30, 1991, fourteen Soviet soldiers were taken hostage.

all of the 4,000 inhabitants within a couple of weeks. Many of the villagers were forced to sign "voluntary statements of relocation." Interviews with these individuals, however, show that the relocations were far from voluntary. Wide-scale looting and burning accompanied both actions.

Operation Ring led to increased violence, not less. It became a clarion call for Armenians both in Nagorno-Karabakh and in the Republic of Armenia. In the fall of 1991, Armenian irregulars fought to take back the villages lost that spring and summer. Fighting also increased along the Armenian-Azerbaijani border and in Nagorno-Karabakh. By early 1992 full-scale fighting broke out between Nagorno-Karabakh Armenians and Azerbaijani authorities.

The Soviet Union officially dissolved itself in December 1991. The Soviet successor states involved in the conflict—Armenia, Azerbaijan, and the breakaway Republic of Nagorno-Karabakh—have for the most part exhibited the same violent, short-sighted approach to communal affairs as their Tsarist and Soviet predecessors.[30] The forced removal of people due to their ethnicity, looting, destruction of villages, attacks on civilians, and hostage-taking are the rule, rather than the exception. A perverse *quid pro quo* marks the behavior of both sides. Hundreds of Azeri civilians died when Armenian forces seized the village of Khojali in Nagorno-Karabakh in February 1992. Little is known of the fate of many Armenian hostages seized when Azeri forces captured Maraga in April 1992. No Armenian was allowed to remain in his or her village when Azeri forces captured the Mardakert region of Nagorno-Karabakh in July 1992, just as victorious Armenian units expelled Azeris from Shusha when it fell two months earlier in May.[31] The Azerbaijani government conducted a merciless air campaign in the summer and autumn of 1992, mostly against civilian targets.

In 1993, the war turned in favor of Armenian forces, and roughly 500,000 Azerbaijani civilians fled Armenian offensives that seized Azeri-populated provinces surrounding Nagorno-Karabakh on the east, south, and west. Presently, the total number of displaced person and refugees in Azerbaijan hovers around one million. Hundreds of Azeri civilians were taken hostage, and many are still being held in Stepanakert.

---

[30]On January 6, 1992, the Nagorno-Karabakh Armenians held a referendum and declared independence. Although no government has recognized its independence, the Republic of Nagorno-Karabakh still bears responsibility for activity that occurs on its territory.

[31]Shusha was the last Azeri town seized by ethnic Armenians in Nagorno-Karabakh. The town fell in May 1992.

Looting and the wanton destruction of civilian property is endemic. Armenians from the Mardakert region found little of their homes after Armenian forces recaptured their villages in late 1992. One Western journalist who visited Mardakert in September 1992 commented that, "The city of Mardakert...is now a pile of rubble. After the burned houses and smashed vehicles, the eye is drawn to the more intimate detritus of destroyed private lives: pots and pans, suitcases leaking sullied clothes, crushed baby strollers and even family portraits, still in shattered frames."[32] Agdam, an Azeri-populated city of some 150,000 close on Nagorno-Karabakh's eastern border, was looted and torched in July 1993 after Armenian forces seized it.[33]

From the beginning of the Karabakh conflict, Armenia provided aid, weapons, and volunteers. According to Karabakh authorities, Armenia was providing between 70 and 90 percent of the enclave's yearly budget in the form of interest-free credits. Some analysts believed that payments to Karabakh constituted 7 to 9 percent of Armenia's yearly budget. After a December 1993 Azerbajani offensive, Armenian involvement in Karabakh escalated. The Republic of Armenia began sending conscripts and regular army and Interior Ministry troops to fight in Karabakh. In January 1994, several active-duty Armenian Army soldiers were captured near the village of Chaply, Azerbaijan. While Armenia denied involvement in the conflict, in London in February 1994 President Levon Ter-Petrossian stated that Armenia would intervene militarily if the Karabakh Armenians were faced with "genocide" or "forced deportation." The fighting during this Azerbaijani offensive, which lasted until February 1994, was exceptionally brutal. International aid agencies and foreign governments were concerned at the low number of prisoners of war registered given the scale of fighting.

To bolster the ranks of its army, the Armenia government resorted to press-gang raids to enlist recruits. Draft raids intensified in early spring, after Decree No. 129 was issued, instituting a three-month call-up for men up to age forty-five. Military police would seal off public areas, such as squares, and round up any one who looked to be draft age. All male Armenian citizens between the ages of twenty-five and forty-five were forbidden to leave the country without

---

[32]Thomas Goltz, "TCG-33 (paper)," Institute of Current World Affairs (Hanover, New Hampshire), September 18, 1992.

[33]According to a Western diplomat involved in CSCE Minsk Group, the action was planned and carried out by Karabakh Armenian authorities. He bases this accusation on intelligence data.

special permission.   According to a report in the influential German daily *Sueddeutsche Zeitung*, the United Nations High Commissioner for Refugees issued an order by which Armenian draft resisters should be given refugee status.

Conclusion

Tsarist, Soviet, Armenian, and Azerbaijani, manipulative government policies that pit one group against the other for political gain lie at the heart of the struggle between Azeris and Armenians.   Both Tsarist colonial administrators and their Soviet successors manipulated peoples in Transcaucasia in an effort to fortify central control.   Perestroika and post-Soviet era authorities in Armenia and Azerbaijan inherited this poisoned legacy, and then simultaneously became both masters and prisoners of it.   They pursued partisan and violent policies toward the respective Armenian and Azeri minorities in their states, which alienated both nations from each other and forced their dependence on the center, namely Moscow.   The government of the self-proclaimed ethnic Armenian "Republic of Nagorno-Karabakh" has also followed similarly violent policies.   The war over Nagorno-Karabakh is fought not only with tanks and artillery, but more tragically with the fates of ancient communities.